D0776930

The Widower

The Widower

Jane Burgess Kohn / Willard K. Kohn

BEACON PRESS : BOSTON

Beacon Press books are published under the auspices
of the Unitarian Universalist Association

Published simultaneously in Canada by
Fitzhenry & Whiteside Limited, Toronto

(hardcover) 9 8 7 6 5 4 3 2 1

Library of Congress Cataloging in Publication Data

Kohn, Jane Burgess.
    The widower.
    Bibliography: p.
    Includes Index.
    1. Bereavement—Psychological aspects.   2. Widowers.
I. Kohn, Willard K., joint author.   II. Title.
BF575.G7K63   155.9′37   77-75439
ISBN 0-8070-2734-0

*To all those who have
lost a loved one
and loved again,*

*in loving memory of
Beth Maule Kohn
and
Samuel George Burgess*

Contents

viii   Contents

Preface

Two years before I met her, Dr. Jane Burgess was researching the plight of the widower, contacting as many groups concerned with the widower as she could find. She was looking for information to give her a common ground that united all widowers regardless of age, family situation, or number of children. As I understood her intent, she planned to use her findings as the basis of a book that would serve to show widowers how others were coping with problems they, too, were experiencing.

I first met Jane at a meeting for widows and widowers in Milwaukee where she was administering her questionnaire to gather information for her book. Perhaps to call her attention to myself, I returned the questionnaire to her unanswered, telling her I believed that grief and sorrow were too personal to put on paper, and that it was really no one's business but mine.

Several months later, she again addressed this same group of widowed persons to report on early findings from her research. I again approached her; only this time, I offered to help her with her research in any way that I could. She accepted my offer with the suggestion that perhaps we could talk about the book over dinner some night soon. Two nights later we did have dinner, and several months later we were married.

It was then that the idea was conceived for the joint effort that our book has become. I picked up the proverbial pen and began to put into words what was inside of me—my feelings, my reactions, my emotional responses to situations that at the time of my first wife's illness and death were almost unbearable. My words have become part of our book, along with the words of many others who participated in Jane's research. Our combined efforts have achieved an honest, open, candid portrayal of what life is like for a widower from the death of his wife to his finding a new life for himself.

Now writing for my wife, Jane, and myself, I can say, "Yes, the dark cloud does have a silver lining." We have reached the point where we have come to terms with our-selves. Three years ago we married and rediscovered the romance that we had enjoyed the first time around. Our maturity has allowed us the happiness that comes from love, respect, and the desire to fill each other's needs—to love together, to laugh together, to face together what-ever life may bring. Writing this book has brought us closer; it has given us a sense of rapport with each other and a purpose to our lives. We hope our book will help others who have gone through similar experiences get back on the path to happiness and contentment.

—Willard K. Kohn

Acknowledgments

It is impossible to list all the people who gave us information about the thoughts, feelings, and experiences of widowers. We are deeply grateful to all of them for their willingness to share their emotions and experiences to help us write a book that we trust will give hope and encouragement to others. Our gratitude also goes to our friends and family who gave us continued encouragement throughout the writing of our book.

Introduction

The idea for this book began with my discovery that there
are no books for a widower to turn to in his bereavement.
It is almost as though no one cared for or understood
about the role, identity, and special plight of the widower
in our society. The few authors who mention the widower
seem to assume that his problems with grief, loneliness,
isolation, and adjusting to change are very mild when compared to problems faced by the widow. One is likely to
read in the literature on widowhood such statements as,
"A widower is at a premium, sought after, deluged with
invitations, while the widow is either a menace or a drag,
a fifth wheel, so to speak." Even prior to my efforts to
research the plight of the widower, my own acquaintance
with men who had lost their wives caused me seriously
to question such assumptions. Certainly the widower, as
well as the widow, is forced to find new meaning in life.
Both must reestablish new social relationships. Wanting
to become an individual again and to reject part of the past
is difficult because one's whole personality is always linked
to the past.

Books abound to help a widow adjust to the changes
taking place in her life. But how does a man feel and react
when his wife dies? What is the immediate impact of death
and grief on the widower? If he is a parent, how will he
manage the many situations involving his children that perhaps were usually tended to by his wife? What about his

social life? His sexual needs? What happens to him if he remarries?

My first attempt to find answers to these questions was made through research, using interviews and questionnaires. The questionnaire was constructed by several widowers to insure that it would pertain to significant issues facing a man going through bereavement, and perhaps eventually going into remarriage. I took the questionnaire to meetings of various single-parent organizations and groups for widowed persons throughout the country and administered it to the widowers who were in attendance. In addition, I obtained names of other men whose wives had died and administered the questionnaire to them by mail. I also tape-recorded several in-depth interviews with widowers. Altogether, thirty-five widowed persons and fifteen young persons who had lost a parent through death graciously and willingly served as respondents for my research. This was a very satisfactory number since I was not interested in making a study with carefully tabulated findings. I was interested in writing a *human* account about the thoughts, feelings, and experiences of the widower. The clinical rationale was deliberately limited because grief and love are emotional, not logical. Though the clinical tone is omitted, the commentary is reliable in that it relates real-life experiences and attitudes to sound sociological and psychological literature.

Together with my research findings, my long-standing professional interest in and investigation of the problems of the single-parent family, and my own experience as a widow for ten years, I felt prepared to write my commentary on the widowed male. An intimate, personal touch is provided by my husband, Willard K. Kohn, himself a widower for two years prior to our marriage.

A few words about the organization of *The Widower*

may be helpful to the reader. The book seeks to provide
a personal/professional viewpoint on the plight of the
widowed male. In order to do this, we've started each
chapter with Bill's account of his personal experiences. My
commentary, directly following Bill's account, serves to
place his experiences into a broader context and relate
what happened to him to the circumstances of other widowers. It is our wish to give comfort and hope to the widowed person. We would like to think that our book will
be a source of help not only to him, but also to the many
other categories of persons who have experienced separation from loved ones.

The first half of the book includes Bill's review of the
agonizing months of his wife's terminal illness and the grief
he and his six daughters suffered when she died. My commentary considers the immediate impact of death on those
who mourn—the disbelief, guilt, anger, loneliness—and the
means for coping. Differences in the impact of death on
a family are discussed in terms of whether the death was
sudden and unexpected or whether it followed a lingering
illness.

Over half of the widowers who contributed to our book
still had children in their care, representing a total of
seventy-two children. We believe this is an accurate semblance of parenthood among widowers in our society.
(Approximately 550,000 widowers with children to care
for are accounted for yearly in the United States.) Therefore, it was important to consider a father's adjustment to
life as a single parent and to include the problems faced
by him as he attempts to reestablish his own identity as
a single male.

The second half of the book brings out its main purpose—to show that there is a silver lining within the dark
clouds of grief. The discovery that men face the same

isolation from their married friends as do women caused us to consider the difficulties a widower may have in establishing new social relationships. After a widower makes the decision that he wants to date again, he may have in-depth conflicts about his sexuality. How a man may cope with guilt feelings regarding sex when he begins to think of dating and remarriage and what he does about his sex needs are discussed at length in the commentary.

The final chapters consider the various thoughts of marriage a widower may have depending upon his age, his family situation, his health, his financial situation, and his personal needs. The variety in ages and family composition of the widowers we interviewed allowed a wide perspective on remarriage. (Of the widowers in our study, eighteen percent were between the ages of thirty to forty-four, thirty-three percent were between the ages of forty-five to fifty-four, and forty-nine percent were fifty-five and over.) The primary reason for remarriage, according to men of all ages, was for companionship and love.

Remarriage for the elderly poses certain difficulties based on age, such as a greater likelihood of ill health and death. But age is no barrier to the delights and happiness that are possible in marriage when the right ingredients are present—feelings of love, respect, caring, responsibility for the welfare of the other, a sense of humor, and the willingness to talk openly and honestly with the other. The final conclusion is that romance and love can be captured in all their glory the second time around.

In order to assure promised anonymity to our respondents, all names used in this book are fictitious except those of our family and the pastor.

—Jane Burgess Kohn

The Widower

Chapter 1

JOURNEY UNKNOWN

We had spent a very restless night together in that hospital room—my wife, a friend, and I. My wife, visibly weakening, was succumbing slowly to her terminal illness. As I kissed her lightly, she opened her eyes, and with what had to be her last bit of strength, she held out her arm to me. I asked if she wanted to pray. No longer able to talk, she nodded. I took her gently in my arms, and we said the Lord's Prayer as we had done countless times before when in trouble. I kissed her softly, and she lay back, resting peacefully for the first time that night. I left our friend with her and went home to our family.

The next morning the phone call came—a voice hesitatingly said, "She's at rest." The first devastating pangs of intolerable loneliness filled my entire being. My children and I had known that this call would come. Still, after a hundred, maybe a thousand fantasied acts, I was unprepared. I remember telling our children, "I'm sorry," while tears streamed down the faces of all. Then for the first time of many more, I felt pangs of guilt; I should have been there. Then anger. I hit the cupboard as hard as I could.

Looking back, I always thought the day Beth went to the hospital was the day *it* started. Now in retrospect, *it* really started in the spring. I noticed that she was taking aspirin more often than usual, but she always blamed it on her aching back. She had put on a little weight over the winter, and we both knew she had been born with an unusual curvature of the spine and had worn a special brace in her youth. Her good days were interspersed with an occasional day of discomfort, and aspirin always helped. Beth's fulltime job as a public health nurse plus her work at home with our six daughters kept her life full of activities—but always more and more aspirin. As time passed, she was content to prop herself up on the day bed and watch television, something she had never previously had time for. February and March passed with only little improvement.

As spring moved on, the pain increased, and we went to an orthopedic surgeon. Due to the problem with her back, he prescriped a special corset that would offer additional support, as well as a board for her bed and a regimen of exercise, which included bicycle riding. April was a good month. The corset and the exercise were helping, and we were thinking ahead about what we were going to do on summer vacation. Once again, the prescription seemed to help for a short while, but then back to the aspirin.

May, June, and the beginning of July were months of intense suffering for Beth. She called it "discomfort." Each day was worse than before, and it took the better part of an hour before she could rise and move freely. She would not stay home from her job as a caseload of needy people were a diversion for her. Constant pain and frequent trips to the doctor were always the same—the x rays showed nothing. Increase in medication helped but always led to more.

One more trip to the doctor—it was July 14, 1972. The examination took very little time. Beth simply was not

responding. Her intake of pain medication was too high.
After going over his records thoroughly, the doctor concluded that it would be best for Beth to go into traction,
and a whole series of tests began.

On July 15, 1972, Beth E. Kohn entered St. Joseph's
Hospital for treatment. She never came home.

The day Beth entered the hospital, she was placed under
the care of a very good internist, a man in whom we had
great confidence. Tests were begun immediately. A complete set of spinal x rays was taken. Again, nothing except
the curvature of the spine showed up. More medication—
this time a muscle relaxant was given; spasms were occur-
ring. Beth was placed in traction—they hoped it would
stretch the spine and relieve the spasms. She also had a
chest x ray, for she was occasionally short of breath.

Physical therapists were consulted along with a neuro-
surgeon who did an electrogram on three extremities. A
slight lessening of strength was noted. She also had her
first session in the Hubbard tank, in which she was almost
completely submerged in water, except for her head and
shoulders. This she enjoyed, for the weightlessness re-
moved nearly all of the pain.

The treatment continued during the next few weeks:
traction, drugs, and the Hubbard tank. The water tank
treatments were often given twice a day. Then the series
of tests began again, because she showed no improvement;
instead, her condition slightly worsened.

They did x rays of the colon, gallbladder, and stomach;
they did a spinal tap; they took a myelogram. Her regular
treatment continued: exercise, the Hubbard tank, and
traction. I would arrive at the hospital, and Beth would
be physically exhausted. An endless stream of friends and

family visitors further exhausted her. I wanted to restrict
visitors to family only, but she would have none of that.
"People who take time from their busy day to see me are
always welcome," she told me.

It was now the first of August, and tomorrow would be
our twentieth wedding anniversary. The results of all the
tests were still negative. There was nothing wrong, but she
was not getting better. Being a nurse, she was sure it was
something exotic. One day, years before, I had come home
and found her in tears. She had blue blotches on her arm
and a slight edema condition, which she had diagnosed as
leukemia, a rare kind. After tests, it was found that she
was anemic and needed iron and vitamins. It must have
been terrible for her, knowing now what it was *not* and,
like me, wondering what it was. She never discussed this
with me, but like most happily married people each of us
knew what the other was thinking.

Our daughters were excellent; they visited their mother
daily. They were wonderful at home as the pressure and
tension were equally hard on them as on me. I literally had
nothing to tell them, but they thought I was keeping the
truth from them. I wasn't. I believe it would have been a
relief even to tell them unpleasant news—at least then they
would have known *something.* They ranged in age from
eleven to nineteen years old. It's hard to understand the
unknown. They wanted their mother home; so did I.

On August eleventh, our fifth daughter turned fourteen;
we all visited Beth. She was tired but very happy for
Claudia, our daughter. The girls did a beautiful job of
showing happiness for Claudia; there was a lot of small

talk, reminiscence, and good-natured kidding. We were a family. Beth's medication was increased again that day.

The next eleven days were devastating for Beth: more tests, repeats of those taken earlier, another electrogram, further weakening of the extremities. The tests were negative. On August twenty-first, we met with the internist. He made only one statement after reviewing all the tests and their negative results. "Bill," he said, "if Beth were my wife I would take her to the Mayo Clinic. I will make the arrangements if you like." We did. At eight-thirty the next day we were on our way to Rochester, Minnesota, and the Mayo Clinic. Before I left St. Joseph's, I received all the x rays, all the results of the tests, and her daily charts. I was to turn these over to the doctors at Mayo Clinic.

We arrived at Mayo Clinic, St. Mary's Hospital, at 2:30 in the afternoon. Three of our daughters came with us to provide company for me and to help with Beth, if necessary. I had mentally built up all types of problems on admission. We arrived at the emergency entrance. The motor home I had rented was too high to get all the way under the canopy. With my help, Beth painfully got to her feet and took a few shaky steps to the door—one more painful step down to the waiting cart. Skilled hands gently laid her down and she was gone before I could get the records I had brought along.

I went to the admission desk expecting to see Beth lying there, but she was already in her room. They took the envelope with all the records, told me that she would be in room 335, and kindly asked me to move the motor home. I could park it on the back parking lot as long as I wanted to. It took me perhaps ten minutes to park the unit, after which two of my daughters accompanied me to room 335. The door was closed. I knocked. In the room were three doctors and several nurses, and tests were being readied. I was asked to wait in the day room. I felt apprehensive but also reassured. She was in good hands.

It was August 22, 1972, our first day at Mayo Clinic. We checked into the hospital at 2:30 P.M. By 6:30 that same evening, they had duplicated every test previously run. There seemed to be a sense of urgency in their approach to Beth's illness. Beth was utterly exhausted and slept restlessly, awakening often with a start. It was around 7:00 P.M. when the three-man team of doctors asked me to leave during a routine check. One of the nurses noted a substantial weakness in Beth's extremities. Her physical strength was failing rapidly. Then the loss of strength stopped, and she started to regain the use of her legs and arms again. Another myelogram was taken even though she was extremely weak. For the first time, a blockage of the spinal column showed up. The doctors breathed a sigh of relief. Here was something tangible. Surgery would be at 8:00 A.M. the following day. Beth was given medication for the night.

My daughers and I left the hospital. We all slept in the motor home on the hospital parking lot. Our night was a restless one: twenty years of marriage and what the future would bring were foremost in my mind.

As I left the camper the next morning, I told the girls to follow shortly. I was in Beth's room at 7:00 A.M. I walked into an empty room. The nurse told me the doctors wanted to see me in the consultation room of the surgical floor. Once again a myelogram had been taken and the blockage was apparent. The surgeon in charge told me that it was apparent that a spinal fusion would be neces-

sary. He said that he had discussed this with Beth and that
she fully understood what was to be done. She was being
prepared for surgery. I looked at the x ray of the myelogram, and he pointed out the blockage and indication of
a degenerating disc. When I asked why this didn't show up
earlier he did not answer, but indicated it was not uncom-
mon. He flipped the light off, and the x ray went black.
It would be a long operation. If there was something I had
to do, I could be gone two hours with no problem; it
would be much longer.

I left, met my daughters coming in, and told them what
I had learned. We went out to find a place where I could
park the mobile home. The nurse at the admission desk
had mentioned a trailer camp a few miles away. We found
the trailer camp and rented a place. I then returned to the
hospital and waited in Beth's room as instructed. Four
hours passed before the doctors entered. Two of my three
daughters were with me.

What followed is the one thing that I wish I could
change. I am a direct person, many times brutally frank.
My first question was, "How is Beth?" The answer, "She
came through the surgery fine; she's in intensive care re-
covering." My next question was, "Is it a disc?" The
answer, "No, a tumor." My next question, "Is it benign?"
The answer, "No, we couldn't remove it all."

Had I known the rules at St. Mary's, I never would have
asked with the children present. I threw my glasses onto
the bed, looked at my daughters, and said, *"Oh God!"*

I immediately asked the girls if they understood, and
they did. I asked them to leave and not tell Judith, the
youngest. At eleven years of age, she could wait to hear.

When they left, I was ready to verbally blast the doctor
as I turned to him. He held up his hand. "Mr. Kohn, I

know what you are going to say, but please listen." Very patiently he explained hospital policy. Because of litigation in the past, a direct, honest answer to any question asked is given. If you ask, you receive an answer at once. Yes, it is at times cruel and insensitive, but if a patient or husband or wife, mother or father, asks, an answer is given. They are told the whole truth.

The doctor continued telling me what was found. While he was talking, the surgeon-in-charge came into the room. With honest compassion, deep understanding, and a real tear, he finished the account of the surgery. After the initial incision and clearing of the area, he was looking at a gray mass on the spinal column. At the sight of the affected area he said he felt a surge of relief, for in appearance and configuration it was a degenerating disc. Almost casually he asked for a pathological sample to be taken to the lab, as he prepared the area for laminectomy and fusion. The report came back—*malignant.* He said that when the report had come back, he ordered a second sample at once. He told them they were wrong. Again the report—"malignant level three." Tumors, he explained, are graded on a level of one through four. This was about as bad as they could get. They called it "metastatic adenocarcinoma of the thoracic spine."

I listened to this from a doctor who seemed to be deeply affected by his own and his team's inability to do more than they had, but it was little comfort. Inhaling deeply, I asked, "How long?" By this time the third member of the surgical team was present. He answered, but it was a very guarded statement. He said, "I have seen them live two to three years." My mind was racing ahead to a possible cure. More conversation followed; most of it had no meaning until later.

"When can I see her?" I asked. "She is in intensive care, and you can see her for ten minutes every two hours," they answered. I had just missed the visiting hour, but they allowed me to see Beth. She looked terrible. They were administering blood and additional fluid. I was surprised to find her awake. "How are you?" I dumbly asked. She feebly answered, "I love you," and fell asleep. I got the hell out of there as fast as I could. I had to be alone. I had many people to call; yet I didn't know how I was going to tell them.

I called my daughters first. I broke down several times during the call. I know it was not my fault, but I felt guilty having to tell them the truth. I kept saying "I'm sorry, I'm sorry," then sobbed uncontrollably. I cried then and many times since. I guess I was lucky to be able to vent the pent-up emotions. The following calls to Beth's sisters and brother, and finally my parents, were the same. I would gain control; then as I talked, the control would erode, and only my emotions would or could talk through the tears. Words, even those meaning to be sympathetic, are cruel when used on the phone. Believe me, I didn't think of that then, but now I wonder if I didn't do a real disservice to my family. I was not with them to share the grief, sorrow, and anger.

During the rest of that day and the next, I was there every two hours for my ten-minute visit. Beth was coming along as well as could be expected. The second or third time I was allowed to see her our daughters came along. Beth appeared to be resting, but at the sound of my voice she opened her eyes. Seeing the girls, she smiled and said, "I love you—all," then added, "Mind your father," and once again was asleep.

As we came out of the recovery room, the surgeon was there and said that he wanted to speak to me, so I told the girls to wait in the day room. I would be along soon.

The surgeon told me that he felt Beth was doing fine and certainly was showing courage and strength. I asked what he meant. He said she had asked about the surgery, and per hospital policy, he told her everything. I asked about her reaction. Once again, with tears in his eyes, he shook his head and answered, "She said, 'Thank you for being honest.' "

I do not know if Beth ever cried, cursed, or broke down. I do know that during our twenty years of marriage she was one of the most gentle, understanding, and loving persons imaginable. She was no saint—we had our disagreements. Her temper when pushed to the nth degree was awesome. But her ability to love and forgive encompassed all who knew her. I believe she was at peace with herself and God.

We left the hospital after visiting hours and went back to the motor home. The three girls, exhausted by the long day, picked lightly at their food. It was hot, and the air conditioner in the unit wouldn't work. I had trouble with the drain in the shower; everything that could go wrong did. Finally I started to laugh, and soon the girls were laughing too. It was a form of relief.

The girls went to bed, and I stayed up to read. It was around 11:30 P.M., and I decided to go for a walk, In the stillness of the campground, I could hear running water. I found that the Zampata River was right behind our unit. The water was a good thirty to forty feet below. It was a pleasant sound; as I stood looking around, lights from the campground filtered through the trees, and one single golden yellow leaf floated down into the darkness and was

gone. Its symbolism struck me. I purposely waited there a
full twenty minutes for more leaves to fall. None did. I
envisioned the leaf, ready for its journey, settling gently
on the moving water. I was completely spent, emotionally
and physically. I went back to the camper and fell asleep.
This was the second day at Mayo Clinic.

It was Saturday, and Beth's sister, Mic, and her husband,
Paul, arrived. It was good to have someone else to talk to.
Mic was going to stay with Beth; this pleased me, for Mic
was also a nurse.

Beth had been placed in a private room. We could do
little for her except give her a sip of water and raise or
lower the bed for comfort. One of the local radio stations
broadcast beautiful music that seemed to please her. She
was gaining strength—but very slowly.

Paul asked me countless questions about the surgery and
what followed. I thought this strange at the time, but I
answered to the best of my ability. As quickly as he had
started, he stopped and wandered out of the room. Beth's
lunch came, and Mic helped feed her sister. Because Beth
wanted to rest, we went out looking for Paul so we could
get a bite to eat. He was in the hall engaged in earnest
conversation with the doctor. Paul, a dentist, had more
than an ordinary interest in medicine. I introduced Mic to
the doctor, and there was the usual exchange of sympathy
and thanks for doing all he could. The doctor left, and I
asked Paul what had been said. Paul confirmed with the
doctor what I had told him earlier. He said I was right in
what I said, only some of the medical jargon was wrong.
The day dragged on. Mic took the girls out for supper,
and it was good for them. Mic had a way of spoiling our
daughters rotten, and they loved her as a second mother.

It was good for me to know that they were with someone who also loved them.

On Sunday I had to leave to go back to work and return the motor home. I had arranged for the three older girls to go to Mayo when I got home. Beth would never be alone during her twenty-nine days at Mayo. This was the end of the third day.

Being back at work was good medicine. It helped block out the thoughts of Beth and the future. It was good to be home again in our own bed, though I really wasn't prepared for it. I must have stirred half awake as I reached out to touch Beth. Then I was wide awake. The whole month she was in St. Joseph's this never happened. I suddenly felt completely empty.

I had the switchboard at work notified that all calls for me were to be put through. It was the second day back at work, about 10:30 A.M., when I answered my page. It was the Mayo Clinic, the surgeon calling. Beth had suddenly lost the use of her legs and arm. She was quickly slipping into complete paralysis. They wanted my consent to operate again—the second time in five days. Surgery would start immediately. I told them to go ahead—I would be there as soon as I could. The oldest girls had my car, and the second car, which their mother had used, was hardly fit, so I called Paul and borrowed his. I arrived about 4:30 P.M. and was met by Mic and my daughter. Beth was back in the recovery room and doing fine. They had performed their second laminectomy in five days. Mic had a room for me at a hotel right across the street from St. Mary's. I would stay there every weekend for the next four weeks.

It was Wednesday morning; I had stopped to see Beth. Suddenly, after nearly twenty years together, we had

trouble making small talk. Then without warning, she said, "I would like to see Reverend Bloetcher," her minister from Granville Presbyterian Church. For once I could tell her good news. I had contacted him, and even though Beth was not an active member, he said he would come to see her. This pleased her. She was noticeably more relaxed.

I began dropping in at any hour, now that I was across the street. Many times she would not be awake, and, with tears running down my face, I would stand silently watching her. Other times, when she was awake, we would talk about the girls. Beth had always been concerned about whether we were doing the right things for them. Sometimes I just sat and held her hand; conversation was not necessary.

Her brief encounters with paralysis had left her weak, and this weakness annoyed her. Having been active and independent, she found it difficult to ask for help.

By the weekend, tests were begun again. Chemotherapy could not start until the precise source of the cancer was located. Test after test again resulted in no usable results. This type of cancer has a prime source. A metastatic carcinoma always spreads from the source and rarely does it manifest itself at its origin, making it difficult to locate. (They located it only after an autopsy was performed—a tumor smaller than the head of a pin in her liver. Even i had been located earlier, the end would have been the same. It was untreatable in the liver.)

Slowly Beth began to regain strength in her legs an arm. Soon that arm was back to normal, but the righ was noticeably weaker. She talked of physical thera strengthen her legs. She started to make plans abou turning home and to her work. This was our tenth Mayo.

The days that followed were endless. During the week I would be at work, and early on Saturday morning I would leave with some of the girls to spend the weekend with Beth. Our friends and family had arranged a schedule so that someone was with her always. Their outpouring of love and concern was a continuing source of strength for the girls and me.

My brother, a radiologist, came and talked to the three-man team, and somehow I knew by what he did not say that things were very dark and Beth's future very short. His conversation with her never reflected this, but our talks were vague and indefinite. He was using his best professional manner to save me additional hurt. He offered me no heroic hope. He cautioned me against expecting miracles. I think that he was trying to tell me that any improvement would be temporary and these surgical procedures might be necessary again and again. I believe that this was the hardest thing he had to tell me.

It was a Saturday night; the girls had spent most of the day with Beth laughing, talking about happier days. I talked them into going to a movie. I would be with Beth during the evening. She was very restless and seemed upset. I asked her if I could help. She paused before she answered, and it seemed to me that she was struggling to gain control. "No," she answered, "you have enough to handle." "Come on," I said, "it's still *we.*" I could have bitten my tongue at this choice of words, but she chose to ignore it and said, "Yes, it's still *we.* I am tired now, Bill," she said, "and I think I'll sleep. Why don't you go with the girls?" I said that I would stay with her and read, in case she needed something. She fell asleep almost immediately. I sat listening to the smooth, rhythmic sound of her breath-

ing. It must have been around 9:30 P.M. when the girls
tapped lightly on the door and came in. I motioned them
to be quiet, and we left her room. The girls were going to
get a pizza and wanted to know whether I cared to join
them. I said no, but mentally I was very happy they
seemed to be enjoying the evening out.

I started back to my room across the street, but for
some reason I decided to go to the chapel. I had been told
how beautiful it was. The chapel was quite dark; vigil
lights blinked near the main altar. A single light spread a
soft glow over a lectern about halfway up the aisle. It must
have been the talk with my brother, the poor choice of
words talking with Beth, or the long endless nightmare
that was barely half over. I did what I am told countless
others have done—I tried to make a deal with God. I guess
it must be the final admission to oneself that all else has
failed. I once more turned to the divine deity.

I begged, threatened, cajoled, demanded, that Beth be
cured. I offered myself in her place. I promised things that
I know I am too weak to deliver. Tears once again
streamed down my face. I denied his existence, then
begged for forgiveness. I did all these things because I did
not want to lose my wife. Searching for an answer, I stood
at the lectern and read passages from the Bible. There was
no answer. I left the chapel. Ashamed of what I did but
knowing that I had had to try, I returned to my room. I
fell asleep again, emotionally empty. My last thoughts
were not "Why me?" but "Why Beth?" I knew of many
people who were less desirable by society's standards; I
knew I could not judge lest I be judged, but I did.

Sunday morning I was waiting in the hall outside Beth's
room when the doctor came out. He motioned me away
from the door. "We will have to start radioactive therapy;

has your wife talked to you about the cancer?" he asked. "No," I replied, "I think she wanted to but changed her mind. Is this normal?" "Yes, in a strange sort of way, it is. Mr. Kohn, people react differently to the fact they are dying—they respond in one of three ways. First, they may go completely to pieces emotionally; they cannot accept the truth. Second, they may accept the truth and never talk about it again; they simply do not want to discuss the matter. Third, they may talk continuously about it in an abstract manner as though it's someone else, not them. It's my guess," he continued, "that, somewhere down the road, she will talk about it with you. Till then, I would not push the subject till she is ready. You have a strong-willed wife; she believes she will beat it. Who knows? The mind can do many unexplainable things." He once again urged extreme caution on my part. "Miracles are rare," he said. This was our fifteenth day at Mayo Clinic. That evening I returned home. It was now a matter of time.

The following weekend brought a nice surprise when I returned. Beth was very alert and looked good. Her color had returned to near normal. She never used makeup, so it was wonderful to see the color in her face and the life in her eyes. My daily calls to her meant a great deal to me, but to see her like this was the best medicine for me and the girls. I had all six of them with me. We had a belated birthday party for Barb and Karen; they were born one year apart to the day. It was nice to have the family together.

The weekend was as pleasant as it could be. We were talking more and saying things of meaning. Beth was full of questions for Barbara about her first week at college: where she was staying, her courseload, and all the things

a mother would ask a daughter who has gone away to
school. It was a good day. Later that same day, Beth and
I sat alone. We thought we heard a light tap at the door.
I got up to see who was there. It was Reverend Bloetcher,
her minister. I have never seen Beth happier to see anyone.
I had told him of her condition. This giant of a man came
in, extended his hand to me, and then devoted the next
several hours to Beth. A calm seemed to come over her as
she talked to him.

The following weekend was a busy one for me. Beth was
leaving Mayo, and I had to take care of all the paperwork
involved: the insurance papers, the hospital forms, the endless red tape that makes things go. The doctors had given
me the name of a reliable ambulance service in Rochester—
a husband and wife team, the wife a nurse. The doctor
asked me if I wanted him to make the arrangements; I
did. I went home that night to make arrangements at St.
Joseph's Hospital. Beth would have to return there for
rehabilitation and additional treatment. When I called the
hospital to tell them that Beth would be back the following Tuesday, I was informed that all the arrangements had
been made by the Mayo Clinic and that our internist had
been notified. What could I say? Expectations were high
at home. Mother would be near us now. We could see her
every day. This was our twenty-seventh day at Mayo.

Monday night I was at home with the girls when the
doorbell rang. It was a very close friend of Beth's. She and
Beth had been in nurses' training together. She also
worked with Beth. After the usual polite questions, she
handed me an envelope. "It's from our class," she said
proudly, "from all those we could reach." It contained
over $300. "It's to pay for the ambulance," she said, with

tears in her eyes. Again, what could I say? I just cried. This was the twenty-eighth day at Mayo.

I was full of anxieties the next day as I waited for the ambulance. I had worked till noon; they were expected in Milwaukee at 1:30 P.M. I waited.

Finally the ambulance came. In it were my wife, a most warm and understanding sister-in-law, the nurse, and the driver. Beth was tired but in good spirits. She was almost home.

It was September 19, 1972. Beth was allowed to rest during her first full day back, then therapy started: the Hubbard tank, therapeutic and bedside exercise, the tilt board to get her accustomed to a standing position. Beth was extremely tired when I arrived each evening. She drifted in and out of sleep unless additional company were present; then she would make an effort to be Beth. It was wonderful for the girls and me to be able to see her daily. No more long trips to Rochester on weekends.

About two or three days after Beth had returned our doctor left word that he wanted to talk to me. Unknown to Beth, I made an appointment to meet the doctor at the hospital. When I saw him, he wasted few words. "How do you want me to treat Beth?" he asked. Before I could answer, he continued. "There are two avenues open: we can go for the heroics with all *that* involves, or we can make every effort to keep her comfortable. The end results will be the same. With the first choice, we will only prolong the suffering. We will, of course, do everything we can to further rehabilitation, but only to the point that it isn't doing more harm than good. Then it will stop. Bill," he continued, "I know that you've talked with your brother Al, and with the doctors at Mayo's. You know the prognosis. No matter what we think, the real choice is yours."

I sat there for a very long time saying nothing; my mind was racing back to the beginning of this nightmare and beyond. "Call me, Bill," the doctor said, and he left. I was alone. I really don't know how long I sat there. My mind was a jumble of mental tangles. Suddenly I was aware that I was at the door to Beth's room. I knocked lightly, entered; only the nurse was there making up Beth's bed. "Where is she?" I asked. "In therapy, feeling fine today," she answered. "Tell her I stopped in as I was in the neighborhood. I'll see her tonight," I said.

I should have gone back to work—I didn't. There was so much to think about and so little time. It would be nice to be able to say I had a mentor whom I could discuss things with. However, in such a situation, one really is alone. There were so many people to be considered—our daughters, Beth's brothers and sister, so many others that loved her. I knew that if I talked to anyone, I had to talk to all. I wasn't able to go through that. I could not put other people in such a position. This was solely mine.

I went home to an empty house. All the girls were in school. I sat in our room which had been empty of Beth for such a long time. Tears rolled down my face. I ached all over. That barren, empty, lonely feeling crushed me. My mind went back to a conversation the whole family had had long before we knew of Beth's illness. We were talking about this very thing. Heroics or reality. Beth had said that if she were in this position, she would want someone to pull the plug. Our oldest daughter answered, "If that's what you want, you pull the plug." It's not always that easy. I called the doctor the next day. "Doctor," I said, "I will not presume to dictate your medical treatment; my only concern at this time is for Beth. I want maximum comfort." "If it will help you, Bill," he replied, "that was our planned course of treatment." I have often thought of this conversation. If I had to, I would make the same decision again.

Beth's progress continued. She was gaining strength. Her treatment was continuing. Her spirits were growing with her returning strength. A constant flow of visitors came—friends, relatives. Her friends were aware of the situation and were lining up people who could spend the night with Beth when her condition worsened.

September was ending. It was only eleven days since our return to St. Joseph's Hospital. Beth was talking about being home for Thanksgiving. "If you're strong enough," I said, "we would all like that, honey . . ."

We celebrated Beth's forty-third birthday on October fourteenth. It was a very good day. Beth was fully alert. My parents were there, along with her brothers and sister and all our personal friends. They came in a controlled manner, allowing Beth rest in between visits. Our six daughers were there. Beth really was in excellent spirits—not a forced effort. I believe she lived for every second while savoring the love lavished on her that day.

The treatments were now leaving her exhausted. No longer did Beth look forward to the Hubbard tank and the weightlessness. The pain had returned. The drugs were strengthened. She must be kept comfortable. It was time for more tests. The prime source had not been located. Beth now mentioned pain in her pelvic area. X rays showed the cancer had started to spread.

On October nineteenth I was called at work and asked to come to the hospital at once. Beth had asked for me. I called her minister. He met me at the hospital. I went in alone. Beth was very alert now. She had been quite de-pressed and physically exhausted. There was no "hello," just a direct statement: "What's going on—people are looking strangely at me. What's happening?" Patiently I explained that she had been very sick the past few days, and now she looked so great they really were surprised at the turnaround. This seemed to satisfy her. I told her that her minister was waiting to see her. I lied and said that he was visiting another patient and stopped in as I arrived. Once again she was pleased, and this pleasure seemed to put to rest her fear that something was going on. Later that night when I visited her, she had forgotten both visits. More and more drugs. But she was resting comfortably. All physical therapy, even her bedside exercise, stopped. She was too weak to take the exertion. Around-the-clock visitors were there. Beth' sister, our sisters-in-law, her schoolmates— what would I have done without them? The outpouring of love for Beth was unending; she was getting back a portion of what she had given. It kept me sane.

The days that followed were terrible. She slipped from good to bad so quickly that it was hard to plan how to behave when visiting. On occasion one had to be harsh and firm to offset the depression. At a time like this, I could not afford her the luxury of self-pity—it would have left her worse than before. If hope goes, all is lost. I was never really sure whether she understood this better than I, and whether she was keeping my hopes up by forcing me to do the same for her.

During the whole period of Beth's hospital stay, the girls were always there. It was getting very hard for them. Beth was losing weight; her color was poor. It was difficult for her to talk. We all kept up a running line of chatter that really needed no reply. A nod of Beth's head was answer enough.

We would go together to the hospital, and after I saw

that Beth was tiring or falling asleep, I would send the girls home. It seemed easier on all of us. I would stay until nine; then the friend who was spending the night would come, and I would start the journey home. I say "journey" because I wanted to see Beth; I wanted to go home to the kids; but we were running out of words to say; it would get no better.

It was a few days later, and the girls had left. Beth was uncomfortable. She asked me to ring for the nurse. Then she asked me to step out for a minute; unquestioning, I did. I really didn't know what to expect.

The nurse told me to come in, but I was not prepared for what I saw. Beth's hair had been brushed; a small ribbon had been placed on one side of it as she wore when we were married. She had put on lipstick sparingly, as was her custom. She was sitting up higher in bed than she had for a long time. I think there was a slight hint of mischief in her eyes, though it probably was the drugs. As I stepped to her bedside, she took my hand and said, "Bill, where are you going to bury me?" I looked at her. She wanted an answer. This was no idle question. I must have stammered around for a while. I needed time to think. I had never allowed myself to put thoughts like these into words. She waited; she wanted to know. My mind was racing, searching for an answer. She would not accept a "what are you talking about?" answer.

"There is an open site next to your parents," I finally answered. Quickly she said, "No, that's too far for people to travel after the church services. Find some place nearer —promise." During the next five minutes or so, we discussed her funeral. I could not believe this was taking place. When we stopped talking, she pulled my hand to her lips and kissed it. We exchanged our love for each other, and I left.

It was the twenty-eighth of October. My parents had come to celebrate my birthday, which was also my mother's. Beth had been alternately lucid and distant; the good periods grew shorter as she grew weaker. I had not mentioned my birthday to Beth and asked my mother and daughters not to mention it either. The day came and went with Beth's not being aware of anything. Time had no meaning for her—just a never-ending blur of faces, things, and pain. The drug usage was at maximum, and still she hurt.

Two days later, in the evening, I entered her bedroom. She was resting fairly comfortably. As was my custom, I looked at the growing mountain of cards she received. There was one in a red envelope, unopened. It was addressed to me. I opened it. It said, "Happy Birthday." By her own hand (that was obviously shaking) she had written, "I'll always love you," and, as if she could write no more, an almost illegible signature, "Beth." Even in her anguish she had thought of me. She had had a nurse get the card and then managed to write her last written words by herself.

She was still resting when I had to leave. Later that evening I called the doctor. "I want things different." He listened patiently, his only statement, "You're presuming to tell me my business." I hung up. That decision had been made a long time ago.

It was November 7, 1972. I had not gone to work that day because Beth was failing. The day wore on slowly. The minister came, but I do not believe Beth knew. Beth's sister was going to be there early in the morning so I could get some rest. It was about 5:00 A.M.—the phone call came. She is dead.

Anger, disbelief, guilt, loneliness, fear, uncertainty. Looking back, it was good that I cried openly, expressed my feelings, for this is all part of normal coping with grief. I know now that what I thought was unique to me happens in part to all who have lost a loved one. Knowing that I was not alone in what I was suffering was of little comfort in my early moments of grief, but knowing that others have survived the pain of the death of a dear one helped me get hold of my feelings.

Nevertheless, there were immediate things that had to be done. All the proper arrangements had to be made for the burial. Friends and family helped, and somehow decisions were made and things got done. I was overcome with the deep concern and love that had been offered me. The genuine sympathy, the willingness of others to help and comfort let me think, "This I can handle; it isn't so bad; I am surrounded by people who care." I got the feeling that the world revolved around me.

My personal grief clouded my judgment. My mind constantly returned to the near past when someone shared these responsibilities. I thought, "It was so easy then. Now I am alone. Why must I alone decide? I need help." In the panic of grief, I decided with my emotions, not my brain.

Eventually, I had to make decisions; sometimes they were wrong. But it was a beginning. Doubt, uncertainty were pushed back a little. Yet doubt, like an actor offstage, was only waiting for its cue to return. The really devastating part of self-doubt is that it strikes not only once but repeatedly, sometimes months later. Thus it was of prime importance that, for a long time to come, I was careful not to make hurried decisions. I asked for help in making decisions about my wife's burial from a good,

reputable funeral director and from my clergyman. I knew
my judgment was shaky—I could not allow myself to be
pushed or hurried.

Yes, the arrangements were made. Somehow I got
through signing the hospital release for my deceased wife.
I contacted the funeral home to pick up her body. I talked
to the funeral director to make decisions about whether
the burial would be from the church or the funeral home.
I had discussed with my wife where she wanted to be
buried, and now I had to contact the cemetery through the
funeral director for burial arrangements. The death notice
had to be sent to the newspaper and the death certificate
to be issued through the county court. A casket, clothing
for Beth to wear, and flowers had to be selected. Pall-
bearers called. The decision whether to have an open or
closed casket when in state, during the burial service. The
minister had to be contacted to arrange for the religious
service. Arrangements as to time for the wake had to be
made with the funeral director. He gave me a list of what I
must do and what he would take care of. There was still
the headstone to be picked out. Then I went home, still
numb, thankful for all the things that kept me busy and
my mind off my grief. I was grateful to the funeral director who assisted me in so many ways to carry out the
wishes of my wife. In time of grief, our conscious thoughts
may reflect feelings of guilt because of things we could
have done for our loved one while she was alive, and in an
effort to appease our guilt we may tend to "gild the lily"
to show our love. I was thankful to have had an honest
funeral director whom I could trust and who encouraged
moderation.

The services were over. I was at the gravesite. I felt alone.
Tears filled my eyes. I cried. For the second time I felt

utter despair, and loneliness overwhelmed me. I was alone, surrounded by family, friends, loved ones. Each of us was alone in personal grief.

Once again, the rituals to follow. I returned home and found the neighbors had provided food and drink. I was offered sympathy—and countless clichés—and I heard myself agreeing, nodding my head affirmatively. But deep inside I felt empty, half a person. My subconscious screamed—"Go home, leave us alone." My conscious mind encouraged people to stay. I wasn't sure that I could handle things alone. Self-doubt had already taken over.

At first I may have been running on reserve strength or numbness to reality. I even said to myself, "Things really don't seem to be difficult; wonder why so much has been said about the problems one is supposed to have when someone close dies." But one day it's there—the self-doubt. I do not know how, for self-doubt is rather insidious: it can start with a series of small, unrelated incidents. But suddenly I doubted my judgment, my self-esteem; and confidence seemed all but gone. Doubt. The indescribable uncertainty and apprehensive muddling of the mind, the ego-shattering destructive emptiness, the sickening feeling in the pit of the stomach. Simple routine decisions become major problems. Delay—wait—check—become the placebo. "Time will take care," I found myself saying.

The funeral was over, routine was settling in, and I was left alone with the reality of my wife's death. In my mind, I went over and over the details of her death. I dwelt endlessly on what might have been. If only I had said this to her, if only . . . if only . . ."

Commentary

THE IMMEDIATE REACTIONS TO THE
DEATH OF A LOVED ONE

Whether the words telling of the death of a loved one come suddenly, without warning, or after months of knowing the inevitable end, one is unprepared—unprepared to face one's emotions. Bill's outpouring of the trauma of his own and his children's living through the agony of Beth's long illness is a message that the death of one loved member of a family is a partial death of all the other members of the family. Part of Bill's self-identity as a husband died when his wife died. No longer was he part of an *us*—instead he was an *I*.

It is never easy to let go of the lost person. Adjustment to this loss requires a recognition of the reality of what has happened, even though one is not able emotionally to accept the loss. Bill's love for his wife was deep and, therefore, his grief was intense. He needed help in living through the immediate phases of his intense grief so he could accept emotionally what had happened. Like so many others in his situation, he turned to his family for help with his sorrow. They cried together; they shared their immediate throes of grief. However, after the numbness of early shock wore off, he felt very much alone. Even his daughters were unable to help him as time wore on.

Bereavement—sorrow—is something an individual needs

to work through. It is a cry for help. But to whom can a person turn in his sorrow, given the practice in our society of denying death and ignoring grief? Friends want to help, but so often they are unable to because they do not understand the grieving person's feelings. It is impossible to be supportive of another person in time of deep crisis without understanding the feelings related to grief. Bill's feelings were real—feelings of self-doubt, anger, guilt, denial, loneliness. His first reaction to the news of his wife's death was to pound his fist into a wall. After that, during the funeral and afterwards, he played the role of stoic. Few understood the deep hurt he was feeling. One of his very closest friends recently said to him, "I really admired you for taking Beth's death so well—like a strong, Prussian type of man who had complete control of the situation."

What will help in time of sorrow? Not reason, for grief is emotional. We must try to understand the feelings that a person has over his loss rather than judge his behavior as appropriate or inappropriate. We must not assume that a person is not suffering intense sorrow simply because he is not showing it. Instead, we must develop a feeling of empathy for that person so that we can truly say we are sorry for him in his loss.

How can we know what grief feels like? It feels like the sense of loss that anyone feels when he loses something very dear—panic, guilt, emptiness, self-blame—and knowing this, we can say to a grieving person, "I know how terribly alone, how empty, you must feel; I am so very sorry for you; can I cry with you?" These words and thoughts give comfort to a bereaved person. Telling him who mourns that it is all right to grieve, that it all right to behave in any way he chooses, listening to him, grieving with him— these are the kinds of supportive behavior that will truly help a person to overcome his sorrow, to gain hope for the future.

Bill worked through his feelings of sorrow, and still his feelings of self-doubt persisted. "If only," he said—two words with which all who have lost a loved one must come to terms. Bill's adjustment to life without Beth was difficult, but it was hastened by his ability and willingness to express his feelings. He grieved openly—a prerequisite to a speedy recovery to emotional health.

To deny or ignore one's grief delays one's return to normalcy. Unfortunately, not every widower has Bill's ability to express his emotions. One young widower, David, for example, was afraid to show his feelings. He commented, "Men do feel the same type of emotions that women do, but don't want people to know it. We are taught that, as men, we must not show our fears." Holding back feelings is not good. Expressing one's feelings can well be a catharsis. Pent-up emotions often can show up in physical distress, such as sleeplessness, lack of appetite, headaches, and other pains of various sorts.

John, another widower, denied his wife's death, too. He admitted, "Many of us try to deny the loss of our loved one. We say it didn't happen as we fantasize and imagine she is still going to return. During my denial of my wife's death, I frequently found myself having suicidal thoughts about joining her. Playing the game of pretend only delays the trip back to reality. I had to tell myself that she was gone; I had a new life to lead. I felt a numbness, and it was not until a semblance of routine set in that the reality of what had happened struck home. To reach this state of acceptance I turned to professionals for help."

Most of us who have lost a spouse have first turned to family members and close friends for aid with our immediate needs, although one should not be afraid to seek professional help, as John did. Realizing that we are valuable to others gives us a sense of self-worth—a feeling that life is worth living. Many younger widowers told me they found that being so needed and depended upon by their children hurried up their return to emotional health.

Our very best therapy for grief and loneliness is found through loving relationships with others. Still, we are haunted by the thought, "What if I can't go it alone?" Yet, we know life must go on.

Chapter 2

LIFE IS FOR THE LIVING

All through our married life, Beth and I had been confronted with problems and decisions to make, but we had always shared them. Now, alone, I wondered, "Am I doing the right thing?" I searched for answers. My mind rushing into the past, I allowed myself the pleasure of remembering how things were. I let myself revel in the happiness of our mutual love, thoughts of making the right decisions forgotten.

Happy events filled my mind: Christmas, birthdays, the children's first day of school, happenings in the home or on vacation, our first home—year after year flashed by in my mind, and always it was "we."

We laughed together. We cried together. We grew together, but she died—and I was alone, and suddenly I was afraid. I was filled with self-pity. I missed having a wife.

When a loved one dies there are so many things that one can miss. At first all are matters of great need. As time passes and the memory softens, the needs narrow down to a few.

Having never left the hospital environment after she was admitted for tests, Beth was absent from home almost five months. The emptiness and loneliness were bearable because there was always the chance, the hope, she would

31

come home, even after the terminal aspect of her illness was known. When she died, the loneliness grew. How many times would I reach out at night to touch, to caress, only to find emptiness and despair? I would hear myself swear, and then, fully awake, I would feel the agony of self-pity. The thoughts of her working in the kitchen, the subtle squeezing of hand as we walked, the soft spring of her hair as my face brushed against it—on and on went my thoughts until sleep captured my conscious mind.

During the waking hours, I had other things to think about. But the slightest incident or thought turned my mind back to her. I had always known what she was thinking by her smile, her frown. There was a real feeling of warmth as we looked at each other. We felt each other's wants and desires. I remembered the warmth of her love for me and mine for her as we watched our first child in the nursery. Love, growing, ever-growing, enveloping all our children, never diminishing, always capable of more. And as the thought "Now it is gone!" snapped me back to reality, I seemed to feel a bit of residual warmth.

As I tried to return my thoughts to my job, my mind had already raced off on another tangent, and I was lost in feeling the closeness we once shared. Together for over twenty years, our world was complete in our oneness. Together our family was planned, born, reared, and now nearly grown. My thoughts went back over our concerns for our children: "Are we doing the right thing; should we try to be more or less demanding; will they be happy; have we been fair to them?" Thoughts covering every conceivable happening with our children were relived.

I have always said to myself, "I want to go quickly—no suffering for me or for those who remain." I think this is perhaps the best way to die, but most of us do not have a choice. We have to accept our destiny, whatever it may be. I wish it could have been otherwise for Beth, and yet her illness was short in time, however long in heartaches. At times it seemed it would never end, but when the end came, it was too soon. "Just one more day," I prayed. "Maybe a miracle . . ." There was so much I wanted to say. I had five months—a short time compared to the twenty years we were married. But I had a chance to say things I had always wanted to say to Beth. I was fortunate in that respect.

Others aren't so fortunate; one day, without any warning, a phone call comes—a loved one has been killed. There might be compensation in the thought that a heart attack is quick and the suffering minimal. But think of the agony for those left behind who didn't have a chance to express their love or say the many things they would have said had they known death was imminent. Maybe they had said angry words prior to their last parting which they now have to regret, perhaps for the rest of their lives.

But we do have a common sorrow to share. I who lost a wife after five months of illness and the husband who lost a wife without warning are now without the persons who made our lives complete, who shared our love, our victories, our defeats, who really cared for us. We are alone, but life continues. We are burdened with the loss for ourselves and our families. We reach out searching for the happiness that once was ours. Death has brought an abrupt end to that happiness.

Absence does not make the heart grow fonder. Absence makes the heart grow sad. After she is gone, it's strange how a home suddenly becomes a house. The warmth and charm are no longer there. The house is there, but without a wife to share it with, it becomes a hotel. Time corrects this feeling of emptiness—time, and recognition that life must go on. Death does not bring an end to hope. Time and need will rekindle hope's fires and once again we can be warmed by love.

Commentary

ACCEPTANCE OF DEATH AND RECOVERY FROM THE PAIN OF GRIEF

Bill has spoken poignantly of the sense of emptiness that pervaded his being. He found comfort, solace, and love within his family after his wife died. Yet, as he once said to me, "A widower may fill his days with his job and his evenings with his family, but when it is time to go to bed, when he is alone, he feels an emptiness, a loneliness, that fills him with despair."

"The first few weeks and months after my wife's death I nearly died with loneliness" is a frequently heard comment made by widowers. The solution they offer is: "Keep active; remain in contact with family and friends; make new friends; join an organization for the widowed. Remember that life is too short to become self-centered and aloof."

Life does go on. Grief is dispelled if we give ourselves a chance. That the road to recovery is long is a certainty, but the length of that road depends upon the person. Denial, self-pity, unresolved guilt, and anger only slow down the recovery of a healthy attitude toward living without a partner.

Recovery from grief requires that we recognize our reactions and feelings and work through them. It matters little how the death of our loved one happened; the pain of grief is there. The important difference between sudden death and death following a long illness is the complete shock of the sudden death with no chance for acceptance or preparation. When Bill's wife died after several months of illness, he and his children felt a sense of relief that the pain and suffering were over for their loved one, along with the awful sadness. Bill felt anger at the unfairness of it all, but not the shock that my friend Tom felt when his wife died after an operation that was supposedly a complete success. "My wife's death was unexpected. We were all on a high at the news that there was no malignancy, and then suddenly, only hours after the surgery, she died. When death hits a family suddenly, the shock and sense of disbelief must be greater although I know the suffering and grief are always immeasurable when a loved person dies. I was left with a deep-seated anger," he commented. Tom blamed everyone for her death: "It's the doctor's fault—he shouldn't have performed the surgery—the nurses didn't give her proper attention—it's God's fault—why didn't he answer my prayers?" Not until Tom vented his anger was he able to find solace for his grief in his belief in God. Like so many widowers, Tom felt that what happened was God's will.

Regardless of how death occurs, suddenly or with forewarning, few are prepared to handle the trauma of losing someone they love. As Al, a sixty-five-year-old widower, said to me, "We need a more thorough understanding of death and why we feel the loss the way we do." Most of us experience feelings of guilt when our spouse dies, and these feelings hang on unless we get our thoughts out in the open: "Why didn't I make her go to the doctor sooner? Why didn't I help my wife more? I could have done much more for her. Why didn't I show my love to her more often?" When we get carried away with such thoughts, we need to be reminded that our spouse was a full-grown adult with the ability to make a decision to see a doctor. We need to be assured that none of us succeeds in being kind, supportive, loving, all the time, nor do we have to. The problem is not with any one individual; the problem is that few of us recognize the fact that if we fail to show or tell someone she is loved today, we may not have the opportunity tomorrow.

I wish it were possible to offer a way to avoid the pain of grief, but no one can suffer for us. Nothing we can say is going to make the pain less intense. But we can find comfort from others who have gone through an experience of grief; the road to recovery can be hastened by listening to the advice given by others who have walked that road.

Bill and other widowers have suggested that when a death occurs, those who grieve must first accept the reality of death as well as the inevitability of death for everyone. Pent-up feelings must be let out through crying and talking with others who are also grieving. In most cases, it is impossible to grieve alone. Being with others who need and love us brings us a sense of security and closeness. It does no good to dwell on how unhappy we are. We must get active and involved with life rather than wasting time on self-pity. Turning to faith in God can help one to accept the inevitability of death and to perceive that life should be lived from moment to moment.

Emotional stress is a problem of great dimension. Most widowers experience great feelings of loss, loneliness, guilt, anxiety, and depression when separated from their wives. Many express a sense of rootlessness. Wanting to become an individual again, having to let go of the past, is difficult because one's whole identity, the sense of who one is, is always linked to the past. How does a man who loses his

wife go about adjusting to the changes that are taking
place both in his life and in his self-image? He must let go
of some of his past. This is never easy. Adjustment to this
loss and acceptance of a changed identity require a recognition of the reality of what has happened as well as an
emotional acceptance of the loss.

As John has already told us, he was unable to adjust
to the death of his wife and turned to professionals for
counseling. It is always wise to seek help from a psychiatrist, clergyman, family counselor, or other supportive
professional for individual or group counseling when depression is so deep that one cannot cope with it alone. This
is particularly crucial when the depression lasts more than
a few weeks.

Depression is usually indicated when one feels dejected
and starts to lose interest in everything—people, work,
family—and thoughts of suicide may also be present. A
depressed person is likely to have a high degree of self-
blame. He finds concentration difficult. Physical symp-
toms may include lack of appetite, sleeplessness, stomach
distress, fluctuation of emotions from wild excitement
to deep feelings of inertia, loss of interest in physical
appearance, and feelings of hopelessness and helplessness
to make things better.

Depression can vary in degree from day to day. But, as
I said before, if it continues, the widower should seek professional help. Many counselors will tell a widowed person
to get involved in doing something. For example, John was
told to get a new hobby or become active in an old one.
He was encouraged to take dancing lessons and, since finding that dancing did provide relief, John literally has
danced his way out of depression. Through his interest in
dance, he has met other interesting people, which has led

to other activities as well. His counselor also suggested that
he find a number of other things he enjoyed doing so that
whenever he began to feel anxious he could find something
with which to busy himself.

John was also encouraged to talk to himself. I laugh
when I think of the old myth which tells us that talking
to oneself is a sign of insanity. Rather, we find that it is
good therapy. John told me that he would tell himself,
"I knew when we were married that one of us would be
widowed some day. She loved me and would not like my
sitting home feeling sorry for myself. I remember how she
always wanted us to enjoy life. She is probably telling me
right now, wherever she is, to find myself an attractive
woman and begin living again."

In many cases of severe depression a doctor may pre-
scribe antidepressant drugs, and possibly sleeping pills for
insomnia. In other cases, therapy, talking through problems with a professional, may be sufficient. John's depression called for both drugs and therapy treatment. The
depression was overcome in about nine or ten months,
but he remained under the care of his psychiatrist for
a year because he had had suicidal notions. John was an
impulsive person, full of anger and revenge when his wife
died. He needed his psychiatrist's empathy—his support,
his understanding, and his encouragement to face the future and make for *himself* a new and satisfying life as a
man without a wife.

Whether or not a widowed person needs professional
counseling, there are other sources of help available. Help
groups have been formed throughout the United States.
One of the largest is Parents Without Partners, an international, nonprofit, nonsectarian educational organization
devoted to the welfare and interests of single parents and

their children. It was incorporated in the state of New
York in March 1958 and now has chapters in every state in
the Union, in Canada, and in Australia. Its program and
activities are entirely the volunteer work of its members.
Other single-parent organizations are sponsored locally
by various church and community groups. A phone call
to a church office, to a local YM/WCA or YM/WHA, to
a mental health association or clinic, or to a public health
office may provide information about community services
and organizations that are available to single parents.

Organizations and programs specifically for the widowed person have been established on both the local and
national levels. NAIM is a national organization sponsored
by the Catholic Church to serve the spiritual and emotional
needs of widowed men and women. Other widow and widower groups may be found that are sponsored by various
community organizations or by widowed persons themselves. One such program is the Widows or Widowers
(WOW) Club of Milwaukee, Wisconsin, organized by a
group of widowed persons who had attended a workshop
established to train them to organize widow and widower
groups in their communities. The workshop was sponsored
by a grant from the National Institutes of Mental Health.
The Milwaukee WOW is particularly helpful to widowers,
since it maintains a ratio of men to women to assure that
a widower attending a meeting or other social function
will find many other men present with whom he can share
his unique problems as a single parent or as a husband
without a wife. Various programs and services are offered
to help members with their problems—emotional, family,
social. However, WOW is primarily concerned with helping widowed persons reestablish a social life.

Volunteer programs for widowed persons also are

funded by the federal government. For example, Widowed Persons Service Programs throughout the country are funded by Title I of the Higher Education Act of 1965. These programs offer a variety of services such as contacting widowed persons in the area and informing them of community services available for their social, economic, and legal needs. They may sponsor educational programs such as lecture series on death and bereavement, adjustment as a single parent, and remarriage.

Contact for grief counseling may be obtained through one's religious affiliation, through mental health associations, and through public health departments. The important point to remember is that people need people, particularly when one is grieving after the death of a loved one.

Once, when a rabbi was asked what solace he was able to give a grieving person, he told of a young mother who had lost an eighteen-month-old son. "I asked her," he said, "if she would have wanted to miss the happiness of those eighteen months with her son in order to be spared the pain of losing him, and the young mother thanked God for those few months of happiness." When we love, we always run the risk of losing that love. It is a chance worth taking. It is primarily the knowledge that we will recover that gives us hope that we will find happiness and love again. It is this hope that can restore our self-confidence, our ability to go on alone.

Chapter 3

MY CHILDREN'S GRIEF

One of the most difficult things for me was not knowing how the children accepted the death of their mother. Because they knew from the beginning that her illness was terminal, I thought that they had had time to accept the final outcome. Yet, even though we knew this, we always hoped that it would be different, that it wouldn't really happen to Beth. As the days passed and she continued to weaken we knew, but the shock of that phone call, the finality of her death—for this we were not really prepared.

I can remember no conscious effort on my part to share my feelings with my children. The horror of the loss was so great to me that I did not feel it would serve a useful purpose to burden them with my grief. But I did cry with them; I did not hide my grief from them. One of the girls told me later that they knew I loved Mother, but the sight of my tears really shocked them. During our marriage, we were open and casual about expressing our love for each other so that the sight of my being completely destroyed emotionally before their eyes was a grief almost equal to the loss of their mother, according to my daughter.

I felt a deep personal guilt because their mother had died. I know I kept telling them that I was sorry. I really was not aware of how they felt; my own grief was so consuming. In retrospect, I think that during a time like this, one tends to think his own grief is the greatest and is not truly aware of others. It is not until later that we realize the selfishness of our own grief.

At the time, it seemed that my older children were better able to cope with their sorrow than were my younger. Actually, however, the younger ones adjusted more quickly to their mother's death. The older children felt the loss more deeply and for a longer period of time. I could not get the girls to tell me their feelings about their mother's death. But one day about a year after Beth died I had been to the cemetery and I came back feeling rather sad and lonely. I asked the girls if they ever went to the gravesite. They all answered that they did not. I am afraid I reacted very badly, making statements that never should have been said. Finally, the oldest girl, through tear-stained eyes, snapped at me, "You grieve any way you want, but we do not have to look at a grave to remember how much we miss and love Mother." They were right, and I have never questioned their method of expressing their grief again.

Commentary

HELPING A CHILD FACE THE REALITY OF DEATH AND COPE WITH GRIEF

Like Bill, most parents must acknowledge, reluctantly, sadly, that they do not know how their children feel about death. They must also acknowledge that they probably are unable to give their children the kind of help they may need to handle their feelings. When a child suffers the death of someone with whom he has enjoyed a loving, close relationship, his bereavement may be one of the most important influences upon his subsequent mental development. Losing a parent in childhood is considered by many psychologists to be one of the most significant factors in the development of emotional illness in adult life. Exposure to death can also be a contributing factor to emotional and behavioral disturbances during childhood. Children do react in various ways to death, and the trauma they suffer differs in intensity depending on age, personality, and the closeness of their relationship with the one who died.

Bill thought his younger children reacted differently from the older ones. The difference appears to be in the intensity of feelings expressed by his youngest daughter, Judy, and two of his older daughters.

Judy was eleven when her mother died. She recalls: "I remember the morning my mother died. I woke up and heard my dad and sisters talking in the kitchen. At first I didn't think that anything that bad could have happened during the night. When my dad told me Mom had died, I started crying very much. All I could think about was that my friend from school had said the day before that my mom was going to die. I told her that was impossible; it couldn't happen. But she was right. How I wished she would have been wrong.

"After that I never acted the same toward anyone at school. During this time I became closer to my best friend. I have known her for as long as I can remember. She listened to me and never told me to bug off. She helped me a lot. I can remember that for about two months every so often I would cry myself to sleep and have dreams about my mom. I haven't cried myself to sleep for a long time, but I still dream about my mom."

Karen was eighteen at the time of Beth's death. She writes of the despair and sorrow she felt through her mother's illness: "One morning in November I got up early so that I could take a shower before going to school. I had seen my father sleeping in his room, but I just assumed that he had had a hard night and would go to work later. While I was drying myself, he knocked on the door, and I told him I'd be right out. When I opened the door, Dad stood there, pale and with pain in his eyes. 'It's over.' That's all he said. I knew that my mother had died that morning after five months in the hospital trying to stay alive while cancer waged its war. She lost and so did we—a great deal.

"The unbelievability was much the same as it had been when I first found out that Mom had cancer. 'She can't die!' 'Maybe they'll find a cure!' 'She can't be dead!' But there's no fooling the facts. Shock and grief hit, but with

all of the things that had to be done, it came slowly. I
don't think it was until the wake that everything finally
sunk in for me. Although many people were there and
tried to make conversation, it was hard not to stand and
just look at Mom. Perhaps worse, though, was watching
Dad.

"We were in Rochester visiting Mom at Mayo Clinic, and
it was then that I first saw Dad really cry. We had always
known that Mom and Dad loved each other, but sitting
there watching my father cry uncontrollably while trying
to tell us what the doctors had said made it all the more
obvious. It also made it more clear how sick Mom was.
During the next five months, I don't remember seeing him
cry again until her death, but I did see the hurt, the anger,
and the emotions which made him withdrawn at times.
Perhaps knowing that by keeping things running smoothly
and trying to be a little cheerful we'd be helping Dad
helped us not dwell on death.

"Those five months were long and short. I don't think
I ever gave up hope that somehow Mom would be cured.
That's why it is so hard to believe that she's really gone.
After the initial shock was over, I'd often find myself
expecting Mom to come home from work or walk in the
door. It made the loss all the more obvious.

"I can't really say that I was withdrawn for any great
length of time or that I tried to tell myself that it was all
a nightmare. I know that for a long time I could not talk
to anyone outside the family about my mother. Her death
has brought me closer to my family. Always having been a
little independent, I find that I do need and enjoy their
company and advice. Having lost my mother, I have also
realized how much I lost. The saying goes, 'You don't
know what you've got till it's gone,' and it is true. I have

always known that Mom was kind and giving, but I never bothered to stop and see how much life was in her or how much she got out of life.

"Although there are times when I still cry because I realize how much I love and miss her, there are also times when my family and I can talk and laugh about things we did when Mom was alive. Life means a little more to us, and the people we love are more important since we have realized how much they do mean to us. God took my mother from us, but no one will ever take away the love she gave to us or the love we have for her, for it is and will always remain alive."

Becky, now twenty-two, very succinctly describes the anger and grief she felt about her mother's death.

"It was a Thursday afternoon, and we were waiting for my father's call. The call came, and it took several minutes for the meaning of his words to sink in; my mother had cancer, and she was going to die. My first reactions were, 'This can't be true, it can't be happening to us, they must have made some mistake.' But there was no mistake, and it was all too true. My mother was dying, and all we could do was watch. In the months that followed, although we never really talked about it, I don't think that any of us gave up the hope that some miraculous cure for cancer would be found, and my mother would live. But no such miracle came, and every day we would see a little more life draining from her. Then finally on the morning of November 7, the call came from my aunt with the news that my mother was gone. Even though deep down we all knew that this call was coming sooner or later, it was still a shock. It just wasn't fair, my mother didn't deserve to die; she was so kind and considerate and loving, and there were so many people who didn't deserve to live; why weren't they the ones to die? These were my first reactions.

"In the few days between her death and the funeral, we all went numbly through the routines that were expected. But it was as though nothing was real—I kept thinking that it was all a nightmare, that none of it had really happened. After the funeral, we had to get back to the business of living a normal life. But it wasn't easy because there was a tremendous space left in our home by the absence of our mother. I began to remember the long talks I had had with my mother before her illness; I could confide in her and know that she understood exactly how I felt and what I meant, but now I would never have this again. I tried to console myself with the fact that I didn't physically need my mother—after all, I was old enough to take care of myself, but that didn't make any difference. Emotionally, I needed her, and missed her terribly. During this period, my sisters and I became very close; we enjoyed each other's company more than ever before. We often would get ridiculously silly just to forget for a few minutes that we had suffered a great loss. This closeness helped us cope with our loss; it somehow made things a little easier to bear. In developing the new relationship between my sisters and me it seemed that we had found a way to work out our grief, and now my father had to find his own way.

"Over two years have passed since my mother's death, and while the old cliché about time healing all is not quite true, time has dulled the ache and the deep sense of loss that I first felt. Even though she is gone, the loving memories that we all have for her will always remain and can never be lost."

As noted earlier, children's reactions to death vary according to their ages. Whether the death was forewarned or sudden and unexpected also makes a difference in a child's reaction to it.

My daughter, Elizabeth, recollects how she felt at thirteen when her father died very suddenly of a heart attack. "I remember too much of the sadness of losing my father. I was at an assembly when I was told to go home. I walked a little slowly at first because I had no knowledge of what had happened. When I got home and saw my mother standing in a green suit with tears running down her face, I knew what had happened somehow, even before she told me, and then I began to cry. I saw my brother sitting with a blank look on his face, and my aunt and uncle, who had come to tell us the awful news, drinking coffee. For a couple days I didn't actually believe the whole thing. I remember crawling into bed with my mother and crying like a baby. The next morning it was raining and snowing, and it seemed as if the whole world was crying.

"It was surprise, disbelief, and anguish. If I could have let myself, I could have cried for days. I still could. It was the knowledge that my mother and brother needed me that helped me pull myself together. We needed each other and we relied on each other for our strength. It was our love for each other and my father that kept us going along with the help of our dear friends and neighbors.

"It was very difficult for me to really accept my father's death because it happened so suddenly. He went to work one morning, and then he died. Maybe if I had cried more, I would have gotten over it sooner. But my mother had to have a serious operation just three weeks after my father died, and my brother David and I had no time to cry for ourselves. We had to keep things going for Mom's sake. I had nightmares about my father's death for many years afterwards, especially at Christmas time.''

When her father died, my daughter was young enough
to accept the reality of his death in a short time. But she
was also very vulnerable because she had a particularly
close and tender relationship with her father. The fact that
she had nightmares for several years indicates that her
adult self was very much affected by her experience with
death as a youth. I am certain that her not taking the time
to grieve for her father, out of concern for me, also had a
bearing on her nightmares.

The complete shock of a sudden death of a parent tends
to delay realization of the finality of death, particularly
for the younger child. Jean was only six when her father
died. At seventeen, she recalls the tragedy of losing her
father.

"One morning I woke up at six-fifteen in the morning
to loud voices and police sirens. When I came into the living room, there were all those strange people in blue uni-
forms and my mother, brother, and sister were crying.
My mother told me that my father was in an accident and
had died. I cried because everybody else was crying, but I
didn't understand completely what was going on. I remember waiting sometimes for my father to come home, but
he would not come because he was dead.

"Now that I have grown up, I still want to question the
reality of his death—it is nice to imagine I still have a
father alive. I also have noticed that I like men that are
somewhat large in body structure like my father, and they
are usually somewhat on the older side. You see, my father
was quite old when I was born.''

At the age of six, when Jean experienced the death of
her father, she was unable to grasp its finality. At that age
she was probably able to recognize the fact of physical

death but not its permanence. To a young child, death is a departure—like the sun that sets at night; it will return when she awakens, so a child looks for the return of the person who died. Unable to grasp the reality of the death of her father, Jean was very distressed by separation from him, and even now, she looks for him in other men. That, after eleven years, she still fantasizes about her father is an indication of unresolved grief. No one understood the deep feelings she had about her father's death. As many adults mistakenly do, the adults in her family probably assumed that she was too young to comprehend what was going on.

I am sure that Jean's mother was no more aware of her daughter's reactions to the death of her father than Bill or I was of our children's reactions. Perhaps there is a kind of emotional barrier that prevents parents and children from communicating with each other about intimate and sensitive areas of our lives. Maybe each is afraid to open the wound for the other, so we avoid the topic. Maybe our silence gives others the impression that we are getting along or don't want to talk. For whatever reasons, most parents know very little about how their children really feel about death or how they grieve. Nor do children comprehend the depth of their parent's grief. Our children said *they* were drawn closer together by the tragedy of losing a parent, but communication between parents and children in the intimate sense was missed. As Becky said, "We had found a way to work out our grief, and now my father had to find his own way."

We are left with questions that need answering. How can a parent know what is going through his child's mind? How can he help his child cope with the death of a loved one?

In order to help children face the reality of death and cope with grief, we must first recognize that children, even at a very early age, will have some sort of reaction to death. We must also realize that their understanding of death will be quite different from ours, for we have much more experience and knowledge about death. However, children do go through many of the same emotional reactions that adults suffer during bereavement—denial, anger, fear, guilt.

It is important also to realize that children act out their feelings in various ways. For example, Judy cried frequently and had dreams of her mother. Becky and Karen faced up to their mother's death at first with anger and disbelief and then with sadness and acceptance. Elizabeth and Jean, who were not aware of impending death, suffered great pangs of disbelief and unacceptance for a much longer period of time.

When children are very young, behavior may even regress. For example, Jack, a widower with several children, told me that after his wife's death, his four-year-old son cried incessantly, refused to talk to anyone, and regressed to thumbsucking. His twelve-year-old son became noisy, boisterous, and abusive of the other children. His fourteen-year-old son, who appeared very anxious, wasn't eating well. Jack noted few problems from the behavior of his older daughters, aged fifteen and seventeen, except that one of them complained of headaches because she was having trouble sleeping. All these feelings and behaviors that may follow the loss of a loved one are normal and should be understood as such. It must be realized that a child's love for a person who dies is as real as the love of the bereaved adult. In the midst of our own grief, it is

important for us to note signs of distress displayed by our
children.

As stated earlier, children, as well as adults, go through a
period of denial. It is difficult for any child (and particularly difficult for a child between the ages of three and
five) to grasp the finality and reality of death; in his mind,
the dead person will return. Outwardly a child may not
show much concern or he may be attempting to deny that
anything has happened. He may think, "I don't believe it.
It is just a dream—Mommy will come back home." Because
he is trying to pretend that this terrible thing did not actually happen, a child may often act as though he were un-
affected. Sometimes a parent may be hurt by this apparent
indifference and feel disgust toward the child when actually this is often a sign that the child is finding his grief
too great to accept and his mother's absence too fearful
to think about. It is very important to explain the finality
of death to a child in this state of mind because, to a very
young child, death is a temporary state. It is unkind to let
him continue to believe that "Mommy's coming home."

Usually adults do not know how to explain the finality
of death to children, with the consequence that many children are left with a sense of confusion. Ellen, at eighteen,
recalled that her father died when she was five and that
death was explained as going away forever. "My mother
made death sound like a vacation that would last forever,
as she explained to me that my father had gone away to a
better place and would never be back, but I should always
remember him. I did not understand, so it was explained
to me as going away forever." This is one way to get across
to a child the idea of the finality of death—a very crucial
step to take in helping a child cope with death. Older chil-

ren find their own answers about the reality of death even though some have great difficulty in accepting it.

Parents may least expect their child to react with anger to the loss of a loved one. Yet, this is very often the emotional reaction of a grieving child. Anger or hostility may be felt against his loved one for leaving him. For example, John, who was ten when his grandmother died, told me, "At first I was angry with her for dying and leaving me. I wondered why she hadn't lived through her illness. I wondered if she died because she didn't care about us anymore. Next I blamed the doctor, and finally I felt it was God's fault. Why did He have to take her? I was angry at myself remembering the times she asked me to do something, and I didn't. I even became angry at my two best friends because they still had a grandmother and I didn't."

Becky expressed similar anger: "It wasn't fair; my mother didn't deserve to die; she was so kind and loving, and there were so many people who didn't deserve to live; why didn't they die instead?" she lamented.

Children have many reasons for anger and resentment. Ginny carried a deep resentment toward her father and went into a very severe state of depression for a year or more after her mother's death. She recalls, "I was eleven when my mother had to have an operation. After the surgery, the doctor told my father there were no serious problems, and we kids wanted to go right up to Mom's room to tell her how glad we were. But it was after visiting hours, and Dad told us we should wait until the next day to see her. That night Mom died unexpectedly, and I blamed my father. I couldn't feel close to him or talk to him for a long time. I know it wasn't his fault that Mom had died, or that we didn't get to see her before she died, but I was so angry that I had to find someone to blame."

Several months after her father's death, my daughter
Elizabeth displayed extreme hostility toward her brother
whom she has always dearly loved. Since David was older,
I consulted with him about family matters, wanting to
spare Elizabeth any additional worries. As a result, she
began to feel left out of the family circle. One night after
behaving angrily toward her brother, she cried hysterically
to me, "David has you, and I don't have anyone—I want
my dad!" Once she had expressed her resentment, we were
all better able to cope with each other's feelings.

Yes, it is important for a child to express his angry feelings. Boisterous behavior and noisy expressions of anger
are signs that he is getting his feelings out in the open
where they can be dealt with and finally left behind. As
John recalled, "After my anger was spent, I was able to
accept Grandma's death as something good for her. She
would no longer have the pain and hurt that had troubled
her for so long. My faith in God's love returned."

Guilt, an emotion very closely akin to anger, also seems
to afflict people sometime during bereavement. Jack, a
widower mentioned earlier, believes that a big factor in
his inability to comfort his twelve-year-old son was his
son's guilt feelings. Prior to his wife's illness, his son had
angrily wished his mother dead. Children often believe that
things happen because they will them to happen. The
angry thought that Jack's son had toward his mother made
him, in his mind, responsible for her death. This could
very possibly explain the boy's unruly behavior mentioned
previously.

June, who was seventeen when her father died, had this
to say about her feelings of guilt: "At the time my father
died I was going to school away from home. For the first
few days after my dad's death, everything was rather

vague. So many things to be done, people to notify, and so on. During this time I know I hadn't fully accepted death, as I thought that any time my dad would walk through the door. I cried, but for whom or why I wasn't sure. My religious background had always told me that death was a happy moment, so why did I cry? I'm sure now that my fears were for myself. I was crying for my own loss, not for my dad's gain of heaven and eternal life with God. Even though religion was an important aspect of my life, I still questioned why it happened to *me*. What had *I* done wrong? For a while I experienced a feeling of guilt that I had done something wrong, and God was using my dad as punishment. I had a hard time dealing with this guilt and can't truly explain how I resolved it.

"There were numerous things that did offer me comfort—friends and family whose presence and concern helped me through my grief. I do remember wanting desperately to get back to school and away from things and places that reminded me of Dad. I wanted so much to forget and to be involved in things that offered diversion from death. Here, too, I felt some guilt in that my mom was at home and couldn't be away as I was. I felt for a time I'd been unfair to her, but in retrospect my mom said I did help. I'm not sure how I helped but apparently she too had her way of dealing with death."

From a common-sense point of view, a child's guilt or other emotions may seem quite unreasonable. But from all that medical and social sciences have to tell us, it is important for parents to recognize that their children can and do have such feelings. It is equally important for parents to know that they ought to point out to a child ridden with guilt that no one succeeds in being good and loving all of the time—nor does one have to be good always. A

child should be told, "It is all right to get angry sometimes! What is important for you to believe is that you did
the best you could, and we love you and understand how
you feel." By all means, we should never let our children
associate illness and death with sin and punishment.
Wouldn't it have been helpful to June if her family had
known of her feeling that God was punishing her so they
could have helped her with her feelings of fear and guilt?

It is most unfortunate that parents often fail to realize
that guilt is one of a child's most common reactions to
death. A child needs to be given an opportunity to release
himself from his feelings of guilt, and often he is not. And
reminders of how wonderful a deceased person was, and
other such things that adults say may cause a child to feel
even more guilty.

The fear of being left alone is another very common
reaction of a grieving child. Such feelings of fear and despair are understandable when we try to consider the panic
some children must experience. James, a young man of
eighteen who lost his mother when he was ten, was terri-
fied and afraid that his father, too, would die. He told me,
"If I heard a noise that was different or if my father would
be late getting home, I imagined that something had happened to him. Sometimes I would just sit in the garage
where Dad wouldn't find me, and I would cry and worry
about what would happen to me if Dad died too. I began
to function again, but never without thoughts about being
left all alone." How can such fears be alleviated from a
child's mind? Young James should have been frequently
reassured by his father that Dad understood his worries,
that Dad's health was fine, that if something should happen to Dad there would be many other people who would
love him and would take care of him. Young adults also

have such fears. Becky, at twenty-two, said, "Whenever
Dad was out late I had a fear that something had happened
to him, too, and we would be left all alone. I knew these
fears were unreasonable, but I suppose they were manifes-
tations of the irreplaceable loss we had suffered when
Mother died."

Just as an adult needs to grasp reality and to find ways
to express emotions in order to cope with grief, so a child
must be allowed some wholesome means for expressing his
feelings. A child should be free to feel his sorrow in his
own time and in his own way. He should not be rushed or
pushed into communicating his feelings. And, most important, he should not be brushed aside in the belief that he
is too young to understand or that someday he will understand. How do we know what goes on in a child's mind
when, in the midst of his grief over the death of someone
he knows, he is ignored? Susan's grandfather died when
she was twelve, and now she still wishes her parents had
talked to her then. "I was sad and felt it was unfair for my
grandfather to die and my parents never said anything
about it, other than telling me he died. I guess they didn't
say any more about his death because they felt I understood that death is inevitable for old people," Susan
speculated.

Children seem to have a way of tuning out information
that they can't assimilate. But perhaps it is better to risk
explaining too fully than to omit an explanation entirely.
In making his explanation, an adult must be careful to
consider the needs of the particular child. Fifteen-year-
old Sarah, for example, told me, "When my grandmother
died, I was treated as though I had no feelings at all. Without any other words, my parents just came right out and
said my grandma was dead and that the funeral was going

to be on such and such a day. I thought my parents came to the point too fast. It hurt me so much. They might have made it come out a little bit easier."

Children should be told the truth, and yet we must understand that a child may not be willing to accept the truth. Twelve-year-old Ruth told me that she was nine when her father died. "He had cancer and they told me that it was better for him to die instead of living in misery. I felt like they were lying, and I didn't want to believe them. I couldn't sleep nights, and I didn't care whether I ate or not. I kept confusing death with sleeping."

A child should be told about death in ways that will make him understand that a dead person's body does not breathe, sleep, or need food. A child needs the essential clarification that sleeping and being dead are not the same thing. Otherwise, the child may fear sleep in the way that twelve-year-old Mary did. When her playmate Sue died, Mary was told by her mother that God had taken Sue when Sue was asleep. "I was scared for months because we were so much alike; I thought God would come and get me when I was asleep."

Most adults realize that the time for understanding and talking is exactly at the time a child has suffered the great loss of someone he loves. We may recognize that a child grieves, yet we often fail to recognize his actual capacity for grief. To make matters worse, many well-meaning people are apt to say to a child, "Be brave, show your family how strong you can be." Being told "Be brave" denies the child his right to show his feelings at the time it is most vital for him to do so. I can remember my own anger at friends who told my young son David, when his father died, that he must be brave, that he must be a man now. He tried; he tried so hard not to cry that he fooled me into thinking that I was a very fortunate mother because my son had come through his father's death so well. Years later, David, in helping his wife cope with her anguish over a parent's serious illness, told her that he would have given anything to have been able to cry for his father. At that moment, years later, he did cry. When caught up in our own problems, it is easy to miss the real feelings of our children. I wish I had done what a friend of mine succeeded in doing. He said, "You have to tell such people to lay off their clichés about boys not crying. I told my kids, 'It's rough on us losing Mother; it really hurts a lot. I cry with my children and tell my eighteen-year-old son that it takes a man to cry." We cannot be reminded too often that children must be allowed to express honest emotions, whatever they are.

Many persons feel that one of the best ways to help a child accept the reality of death is to take him to the wake or to allow him to view the corpse. Nothing may be further from the truth. The actual impact of this experience upon a child will, of course, vary from one child to another, depending upon the age of the child, the relationship of the child with the deceased person, the emotional needs of the child, and the child's personality. Children may get some positive benefits, but children also may be psychologically harmed. For example, seeing a body lying in state may reinforce the notion of death's being the same as sleep. Nine-year-old Warren told me, "My family made me go to my dad's funeral, and it seemed like my dad should wake up if he loved us. He looked just like he was sleeping. I saw my father's dead body in nightmares for a long time. I hate the idea of dying."

I have talked to many young adults, including our own children, about funeral practices. I find that most young

people who have lost a close family member or friend
found the wake distasteful and were angered at being
forced to go through their "performance." My daughter,
Elizabeth, recalls her own distaste about her father's
funeral: "The service was very brief, and I remember telling Mother to quit crying while my tearless brother and I,
stone-faced, sat beside her. I wish funerals could be omitted, because seeing my father dead is not the best way to
remember him. I would much rather remember the times
when he would come in the door with a package of
smoked fish from Port Washington or how much fun we
had at Christmas when we would all go out and get our
tree and trim it and then stack the presents under it. I
would rather remember him as he was on the Saturdays
when we would sneak out quietly, early in the morning,
and paint pictures of the nearby lake and the ducks. Or
how he used to squirt me with the hose when he watered
the grass, or how he'd wink at me when he would usher
in church, and we would pass the collection plate back to
him. Or how we would go whizzing along, sailing in Lake
Michigan. I wish over and over that my last view of my
father had been of him like this instead of lying there in
a coffin looking so unnatural."

Bill's daughters also expressed the wish that they could
have been spared seeing their mother lying in state. "Mother wouldn't have wanted anyone to see her looking like
that, and we didn't need to go through that wake to realize she was dead," commented one of the girls to me.

While concluding that the funeral service itself was comforting as a memorial, the typical response of college-age
people is that, "The wake served no useful purpose for us."

It is the parents' choice whether or not to have their
young children attend a wake or a funeral. We know our

children best—and we should not be afraid to break with
tradition. If we think that our children will be negatively
affected by viewing a dead body, or that our children op-
pose the idea of a wake, we should support our own immediate family's needs and wishes. There is no assurance
that an open casket and a long-drawn-out wake will
provide the positive function it is supposed to. A closed
casket and a beautiful memorial service to honor the dead
may serve a much more positive function. What is really
needed at this time is loving conversation about the person
who has just died.

But how can parents communicate in the way they
should with their children? The widowed persons I have
talked with have found, as Bill and I did, that although
they tried to discuss death with their children it was very
difficult and in many instances they were unable to initiate
conversation. Typically, a father of several teenage chil-
ren said, "They just seemed to accept death. They did not
grieve openly after the funeral. I have discussed their
mother's death with them a few times, and they do not
show any emotions. I wish I knew how to help them express their feelings." Another father of a seven-year-old
said, "Billy uses his mother's death as a sort of crutch—
he seems to be looking for sympathy everywhere. Yet I
can't reach him." The father of a three-year-old child
told me, "It is very difficult to explain to a young child
so dependent upon his mother what these changes are all
about. Jimmy is hostile to me and seems to think I am
in some way responsible for his feelings of being aban-
doned by his mother."

We cannot generalize about the best way to help our
children or ourselves cope with the fact of death, for
everyone's problem is unique and the thought of death

appears as a threat to most people. Thus it is not surprising that most parents put off the thought of talking about death to their children: they stall until faced with the issue. Yet, parents should not wait until the death of someone to whom the child is close. When learning about sex, the trauma of the onset of puberty is much smoother if the child has been told about his or her sexuality in a loving and open manner; similarly, the trauma of death can be softened through conversation between parent and child prior to the experience. If a child sees that his parents are comfortable about discussing death with him, he will be more at ease too.

Recently a good friend of mine died of cancer. Her three young children had been told about her impending death months before she died. Before my friend died she told me her most comforting thought was that she and her husband had been able to prepare their children for life without her presence, to accept the reality of death, and to put their trust in God's way of doing things. The children are lonesome and miss their mother, but they have not suffered the trauma of children who must face the shock of death unprepared. Their father says, "I've not had any serious problems with the children. I'm sure it is because my wife gave her children the opportunity to share their anxieties and fears with her while she was around to comfort and assure them. We had time to come to terms with death before it happened."

Marie, a student of mine, told me that she also is thankful that she had time to prepare for her mother's death: "If it wasn't for those six months I probably would not view her dying as the preparation it was for me. I questioned why it was her and kept thinking things would work out and my mom would live. As time went on, my mother helped me to accept the fact that she was dying. We talked together, and we cried together. Never before was I so close to my mother. I am so thankful that I had the chance to be close to her. She taught me so much through her dying."

But, you might ask, how can I talk about death with a child if I haven't come to terms about death with myself? The answer is, of course, that to tell a child about death requires also that we are sure about our own feelings about it. Few people have reconciled themselves to the fact of death. Perhaps it is not truly possible to accept its reality until one has himself experienced the death of a loved one. As parents, we ought to do what we can to break the chain of avoidance of the topic of death so that our children can grow up freer from unrealistic thoughts about it. Children who have already experienced the death of a parent will undoubtedly be better prepared to cope with death the next time they must face it. Richard assures of this as he comments: "The first several weeks after my mother died I missed her a lot. I would catch myself thinking about something that I should go home and tell her about, only to remember she was no longer there. It wears off with time, and a new pattern of life is formed to adjust for the missing member of the family. I know that I still miss her, but after a year it is not the same anymore. I have learned that death is a necessary part of life. My advice to anyone who loses someone he loves is to chalk it up to experience. We are created of dust and we will return to dust. What does it matter how or when? This is the reality of death. I look at death in a much different light now than I did before. The pain is disappearing, but I don't believe it will ever disappear completely. I have lost a very important part of my life, but from that loss I have gained a much greater understanding of death and respect for life."

To tell a child about death requires that we are sure about our own feelings. We must not try to give an explanation about death that we cannot accept ourselves. Unless we discuss death candidly with our children, they cannot learn that death is a reality. Communication that is clear and open is vital if we are to help them cope with their grief. However, communication among family members or friends is in many ways a "touchy" matter because it not only involves speaking, listening, and really hearing, but it also involves emotions. Communication is a sadly neglected art in many families, and given the highly emotional overtones when illness and death are involved, it is understandable that in times of crisis, when talking is so very important, many people are helpless in dealing with each other's emotional needs. Bruce, for example, said, "While my mother tried to shield our family from the knowledge of her great suffering, it was very apparent. I could not wish this type of agony on any living being. As I look back on my treatment of my mother with regard to hospital visits and general conversation, I wish I could have helped her by providing some kind of emotional release. I seldom talked to her about her pain. Now I think I should have been more direct. I was avoiding her in a sense because I didn't know how to react to her suffering. When she died, I know that not only was I relieved that she would no longer suffer, but I was relieved that I would not have to cope with my own inability to communicate with her."

What should adults do to help a child through the trauma of bereavement? We should assure a child of our presence and love. Particularly in the early periods of grief, a child needs every possible assurance that he is loved. This will make him feel more secure. We should verbalize our caring and show him in all ways that we care. We should try, without being pushy, to get the child to talk about his dead loved one. We must give him every opportunity we can to review memories of things he did with his loved one. We should refer to past experiences to make it easy for the child to reminisce. For example, Bill and his daughters frequently laugh together over past experiences. "Remember how Mother always forgot the salt in the meat loaf, or remember the picnic we had, or remember how Mom used to fix us if we didn't straighten out our rooms?" Any way we can think of that brings the dead person into the conversation will do. And we shouldn't be afraid to cry with our child. For him to see that his parent hurts, too, will make him feel more free to express himself. It is more frightening to a child to be sent away than to see an adult cry. We shouldn't be hesitant about causing tears. Bill cried with his children, giving them an opportunity to cry and release their feelings. It is not good for anyone to bottle up grief. This is what happened to my children. Unwittingly, I spared them my tears, and they, because of my illness shortly after their father's death, spared me their tears.

On the other hand, a child should not be urged to display unfelt sorrow. This could make him feel confused or hypocritical. It is also important *not* to convey to a child that deep sorrow is a fearful thing or something bad. Rather, it is good to point out that sorrow is mainly being sorry for ourselves because we miss the person who has died. Ron, for example, said, "Actually, many of our sad feelings are selfish feelings and pity for ourselves because we miss the person who died so much. They are *I feel* rather than *he feels* emotions. Too much self-pity does nothing but hurt everyone involved. Nothing can be accomplished by it. When we lose someone we love, the most important thing is to not sympathize too much with ourselves. We shouldn't feel resentment about a death. We can thrive on the opportunities and happiness we have had in knowing and loving this person and keep this part of him alive in our memory." In keeping with one's religion, a parent may want to assure a child that the dead person is safe in God's care.

Children have a deep need for a sense of emotional well-being. When all else fails to end a child's state of confusion and feeling of insecurity, he may find some reassurance and insight into his feelings about death by reading a good book. Among the many good children's books dealing with death is Marjorie Rawlings's *The Yearling,* a story of a boy's devotion to a pet deer and his deep sorrow when the deer has to be shot. The boy's father cannot spare his son the pain of losing his beloved pet, but he helps him understand the reason for the pain and gives him the courage to bear it.

There are many ways to help a child cope with grief. The suggestions offered here are not the only ways to do it. But no matter how one chooses to help a child face the death of a parent, it is *very* important that a child be allowed to share in the family's grief. A child should not be sent away to a neighbor or a friend during the periods of preparation and mourning. Dislocation of a child at the time of death may intensify his feeling of loneliness and increase the difficulty of his adjustment, as happened to thirteen-year-old Bobby. As he told me, "I really didn't know that my father was dying. No one really told me.

I guessed. I wanted to catch up on all the time we had been missing since he got sick, but I was constantly told to go to someone else's house. I felt in the way and left out, and for a long time, I couldn't believe that my dad was gone."

A child needs to know that life is precious and that death can come to anyone at any time. A child needs to be reminded that the dead individual can be kept alive in his own mind by memories of that person. A child who feels loved by his family will be better able to develop a healthy adjustment to death.

Chapter 4

IT'S A FACT—MEN ARE CAPABLE OF PARENTHOOD

Like most fathers, I had had little to do with many of the day-to-day aspects of child care while my wife was alive. Now, suddenly, I was fully involved. It was up to me to fulfill our children's physical needs, as well as to supply the love, understanding, and comfort they would need.

The adjustment to being a single parent, however, was not too difficult for me, partly because of the circumstances of Beth's death. During the long months of her illness, the children and I became used to her absence; we thus became conditioned to her final absence. Also, prior to her illness, Beth had worked full-time, and so our daughters already had shared the responsibility of the home and meal preparations. When Beth was admitted to the hospital, we just continued to function as we had been doing for many years.

The ages of our six daughters ranged from eleven to nineteen at the time of Beth's illness. I was not aware of any specific adjustments the girls had to make. They seemed to realize what we were all going through and did their best not to add to our unhappiness. Beth's illness had brought us all closer together. We had been a close-knit family before, but, now in her absence, they came directly to me with the everyday problems that occurred.

I did not have to make any conscious effort to be available. When they wanted to talk, we talked. My oldest daughter was elected to be their spokesman for important problems, but ordinarily we dealt directly with each other, one-to-one. I am certain the younger girls confided in their older sisters about their intimate needs and problems—one of the many advantages of a large family.

Functioning as the confidant was a new role for me. Suddenly my opinions became necessary. I was important to them now. There were no earth-shaking problems. The common, everyday variety were the most frequent. I found that I had to listen and that most of the time they had their own solutions to offer. They just wanted a sounding board for their solutions. When Beth was alive, they went to her with their daily or personal problems, but important decisions were always made by both of us. Perhaps this is why the transition into the single-parent role was rather simple for me. They were already accustomed to my involvement in their lives. I tend to be autocratic and believe that a father should play a role in childrearing. I have kiddingly told my daughters that I couldn't afford to run a democracy in our home because the first thing they would do would be to vote me out of office! Seriously, after Beth's death, I did not have any major complaints from the children as to how we were managing as a single-parent family.

Because of their ages, no special arrangements were necessary to take care of them. We were twice blessed by the availability of Beth's sister, Mic, and my mother. Both of these gracious ladies had tremendous rapport with the girls before their mother died, and this closeness was a source of strength to them afterwards. Shortly after Beth died, Mic made a point of thanking me for allowing her to remain so very close to the girls. I was thankful and honored that she wanted the closeness between herself and my daughters to continue. I certainly had no intention of coming between this relationship. I may have given her this impression because in the final days before Beth's death I withdrew myself from everyone. Without the knowledge that my daughters had such love and understanding from our family what would I have done? Even now, after four years, Mic and my mother are a main source of love and companionship for the girls. We who have lost a loved one must allow those who also loved to be needed.

There was little change in the routine of the family's normal activities. I always had been reasonably interested in my daughters' progress in school. Beth's position as a public health nurse at the schools gave me a personal acquaintance with most of the teachers, and this was an advantage to all of us. My daughters received nothing but support from their teachers during their mother's illness and after her death. Spring concerts, fall concerts, and school plays were attended in the same manner as before. I continued very much as I did before my wife died.

I set the limits for my children regarding what we ought to expect from each other. Responsibility for carrying out certain duties and regulations was based on their ages. For example, when I was gone from home, the oldest daughter present would be in charge of the daily routine. This, of course, was not accomplished without some testing of authority. However, I am not suggesting that the burden of household responsibilities should be carried by the oldest child. To lean too heavily on older children can rob them of a normal life. The care and welfare of children are the parent's obligation, not the oldest child's.

My overwhelming satisfaction with my daughters'

cooperation with me bears repeating. As time went on, my oldest girl assumed more of the responsibility, and I found myself turning to her for help more frequently. As a consequence, she did develop a feeling of possessiveness toward me. But this did not become the problem it might have because I was careful to assure my daughters that I had my own private life to lead, too. If I would decide to go out for a few hours in the evening, I would tell them that I was going and when they could expect me back. They never did question as to why I was going out. In retrospect, I might have told them, for they, too, were lonely. We all missed *her* so much. Time passed, but the loneliness didn't disappear, only the intensity.

After four or five months, the girls seemed to be back in their normal routine, and I had my first date. When they heard with whom I was going out, they were glad, for they wanted what would make their father happy. As for me? I was back on the road that was to lead me to happiness once again.

Commentary

THE FATHER'S ADJUSTMENT TO LIFE
AS A SINGLE PARENT

When I first met Bill, I thought his very apparent ability to relate to his children at an emotional, as well as at an intellectual, level was some kind of exception to the myth that men are providers, disciplinarians, and not parents in the emotional sense. But after discussing "parenting" with many other widowers, I know that, when given the opportunity, men can become parents in the fullest sense of the word.

Being a parent is one of the most awesome, difficult, responsible roles played by anyone. The problems encountered are many and varied within each family circle. It would be nice if it were possible to establish some neat formula for parenting that would work, but it is not possible. We can, however, learn something from the experiences of others.

Bill had rather smooth sailing as a single parent for several reasons. When his wife died, his children were of ages that did not present a child-care problem. They were already trained to take over much of the household care and cooking, as their mother had worked outside the home and needed their help. And Bill had always been very much involved in his children's daily lives. In addition, his mother and sister-in-law continued to give his daughters emotional support.

73

Bill, as well as most of the widowers I know, feel that the loss of their wives has brought them closer to their children. This, of course, will depend somewhat on the ages of the children. Men with very young children may find that their relationship becomes more strained. They may find that their children seem insecure and appear confused about the changes. Men with children between the ages of eight and thirteen may find a relationship which is considerably closer—most problems being easier to resolve when children are beyond the age of ten. Generally, widowers find their children do come to them with the problems they previously took to their mothers.

Many of my widowed friends find themselves becoming more actively involved in doing things with their children. As one father said, "I must confess, that I used to let my many outside activities take me away from home too often. Now I spend more time at home and I'm really getting to know something about my own children. It's great!"

Most of my widowed friends say their children have become more independent, and the older children more supportive, since their mothers' deaths. Typical of this is the comment: "My children have taken more responsibility for making decisions that concern themselves, seem more reliable in carrying out my wishes, and are assuming more responsibility, generally, for our everyday living together."

While Bill had good communication with his children, many fathers wish for more communication. For example, Rudy told me, "Communication is carried on fairly well; however, it's hard for my daughter to tell me girlish things and difficult for me to understand the female way of logic at age thirteen. This is my greatest frustration. The boys I can handle well."

A father often feels awkward dealing with his daughters' needs. Many fathers are concerned about explaining sex to their daughters. As Dick commented, "Mom used to be their principal advisor. Now I depend on my wife's sister to talk to my daughter about personal matters." Bill hoped his daughters would consult their Aunt Mic for sex information if they didn't feel they could come to him. However, Bill has never been shut out from conversation about sex for he and his wife were very open in talking about sexual matters to the girls. Childbirth, premarital pregnancy, rape, birth control, and the like have been discussed thoroughly.

It is true, unfortunately, that most parents—mothers *and* fathers—fail to give their children the kind of adequate sex education they need. Widowers are no exception, but those that I know are concerned about the issue and are trying to find a source of information for their children. The most likely source for sex education, of course, is the school, for many parents lack the knowledge regarding the physiological aspects of sex and are unable to cope with the emotional aspects of sex for themselves when it comes to talking to their children. For the first time, as a single-parent father, the widower may be confronted with concerns about his children's sex education, for previously, this had been his wife's concern, especially in the case of daughters. This is the time to start—his children will now turn to him if he keeps the communication open.

Most children seem to sense the importance of cooperation when left with one parent. Generally, the widowers I have talked with have had the same response from their children as Bill did. "Our children are contributing more to the physical maintenance. They try to clean their own bathroom, vacuum and dust, and I am trying to teach them cooking and shopping. This is still a messy place, but full of love," exclaimed Harry. Another said, "They are great. We split up our chores." A father of a seventeen-year-old daughter said, "She is really something special; from a little scatterbrain she is now assuming most of the responsibility of keeping the household together."

Little change in a child's school performance (except for the better) has been noted by my widowed friends. These fathers said that the teachers, for the most part, were aware of the state of bereavement and were supportive and helpful to the children as they adjusted to the changes taking place in their homes. Many fathers told me they had become more involved in such school activities as attending PTA meetings and consulting with teachers. I remember Tom remarking, "I had never gone to a PTA meeting before, and I felt as strange as hell the first few times. But now I enjoy going, and my kids think it's great."

Cutting down on activities is, of course, a simple adjustment to the reality of life for a widower with children. But this is not to say that every widower is satisfied or happy with the necessary adjustments. For example, Ralph said, "I had to cut down on the volume of my professional and community activities upon becoming a single head of a household. I found that I began to regret the need to re-align my resources. In fact, I must admit that I find myself resenting it."

I think that the man who elects and enjoys his role of single parent is probably very frequently one who already has been performing it in part. This is the key, as demonstrated by Bill, as to whether or not a widower has been involved in child care prior to the death of his wife.

Bill feels very fortunate that he did not have any child-care problems. But for the widower left with very young children, the problems can be monumental. When surrounded by supportive family and friends, the trauma can be lessened; but unfortunately my friend Jim, a young father left with three young children, did not have this kind of help: "When my wife died, my children were fourteen months, three, and eleven years of age. In the help field, it would have been nice if my relatives had helped. Thinking, I suppose, that I would make it anyway, they never did. This was tougher than hell. My wife's brothers and sisters crossed me off shortly after the funeral. They thought I would go right out and find myself another wife to care for my children. The problem of finding babysitters and someone to watch the children was like a nightmare. This has been a do-it-yourself project since my wife's death."

Problems of this sort vary from one family to another and there are no easy answers. But it *is* very important not to panic. Tom, a father of three, said when his wife died the situation was chaotic. A relative came for the first week. "Frankly," he said, "it was a relief when she left because then we could do things by ourselves and get a routine established without my wife. I was more fortunate than most widowers—I was able to find full-time help in the home. She did not stay nights nor cook the evening meal. I did that with the help of my girls. They were fantastic in pitching in with various household routines. But it takes time and patience to take over the role of a wife and mother."

When problems become overwhelming, it is important to ask others for help and to remember that parents and other relatives offer only stop-gap solutions. Most of our widowed friends argue against a hurried marriage in an attempt to solve these special problems of child care and housekeeping. It is better to turn to various social services that are available in most communities for special assistance. A call to a United Community Services Agency can give you a listing of various specialized services in your area, such as:

Preschool Nurseries. These provide various types of child care for the very young child.

Child & Family Centers. These offer parent education, preschool education, and day-care services; nutrition programs, transportation to and from the centers, medical, dental, and psychological services.

Public Health Services. A call to the city or county public health department in your area should provide advice and resources regarding many types of health problems.

Single Parent Organizations. Solo Parents, Parents Without Partners, Widows and Widowers—all are organizations that may be sponsored by and contacted through churches, the YM/YWCA, and the YM/YWHA. Some of these groups are listed in the telephone book, and meeting dates are included in local newspapers. Such groups provide information that may help single parents cope with problems in caring for children, as well as with personal problems.

Probably the most difficult question facing widowers is how to preserve their own individuality and independence, as well as be the best possible father to their children. "How do I remain independent without my children thinking I ought to do things differently?" asked one widower. Another asked, "Would my children resent my association with a woman?" One man said his younger children seemed to resent most activities that took him away from home, while his teenage children worried about his getting married again.

On the other hand, many other widowers, like Bill, found that their older children were happy to see them engaging in outside activities and beginning to date. I recall a conversation I had with the son of a widowed friend. The young man said, "I kinda got a kick out of my dad. He acted like a young kid about eighteen years old. First he went to a couple of meetings of Parents Without Partners. You know, he had to be a good father now. And then he started going with a lady who used to be a good friend of my mother's. It was fun seeing him act like a lovesick puppy. When I think back after my mom died, I remember wondering when this old duffer was going to meet someone new. Dad was forty-two when Mom died, and I surely didn't want him to live alone."

Some widowers have told me their children tried to prevent any new attachments at first, sometimes out of loyalty to or love of their dead mother, some out of possessiveness of Dad, or some in plain resistance to change. And it is possible that a child may genuinely believe that remarriage at a particular time with a particular person is not or will not be good for the parent. Perhaps it might be good to tell our children that we don't have to ask their permission to date again or to remarry.

"Bring the children into your plans, but don't let them dictate. Be fair, but firm. They must participate in the everyday operation of the home. They must know that you value their views. They must know that you do have a life of your own to live, in addition to your role as father," concluded Tom.

Many of our widowed friends have expressed the same

view as Bill's: "We must fulfill our children's physical needs, as well as supply the love, understanding, and comfort they need. We do not have to ask our children's *permission* to begin once again to seek fulfillment of our needs for companionship, sex, and love."

Chapter 5

LOOKING AHEAD

The people who rushed to my side during the first weeks of my grief almost as quickly left me. "We don't want to interfere," they would say. But what they really meant was they wished to return to their *normal* way of life. Continued close relationship with the grieving person does not constitute a normal way of life, and I was no longer a member of their paired world. Perhaps, too, I reminded my friends of the inevitability of death—something they would rather not have to think about. I was a living reminder that death will happen to them and to their loved ones some day.

Friends with whom my wife and I had frequently exchanged visits no longer invited me to parties unless, perhaps, for a family dinner with my children. Fellow members of my bowling team cheerfully might say to me, "Boy, you don't have to rush home," or, "Nobody to keep tabs on you now, you lucky guy, you can really howl." But I noticed they did rush home, and I sat alone at the bar. I was still welcomed into my closest friends' homes, but suddenly my buddy's wife, whom I had known since high school days, greeted me like a casual friend and then disappeared, leaving me to visit with her husband, appearing again only when I was ready to leave. She must have felt uncomfortable with a lone male guest, for when I later appeared with a date, she greeted me with open arms —welcome back into the paired world!

For years, it had been customary for verbal invitations to be issued by one wife to another. Now when invitations came, they were always from the husband. Sometimes I received such a telephone call from a male friend, only to find when I arrived that the wife was out for the evening. After all these years of sharing good times together as couples, what was so different? I couldn't believe I had now become a *threat* of some kind to other men. Me— lonesome old Bill—now a handsome, debonair threat?

Rather, I was a victim of myths: single men have it so much easier than women; widowers never feel lonesome, they get invited to parties; everyone wants an extra man around when the Saturday night group meets. The truth is that I, like most widowers I know, was victimized as much by the fifth-wheel syndrome as any widow. I found myself an outcast in a couple-centered social world. Furthermore, I feel that a widow has certain outlets to escape social isolation that are not usually available to the widower. Widows seem to entertain friends more readily, probably since this most likely has been their traditional wifely role, bringing social life to themselves. I always relied on my wife to plan our social life. After she died I felt very inadequate about having people over for parties and get-togethers. Until I remarried, I did no entertaining except for my all-male poker club. Women also seem to be better able to call each other on the phone and talk things out than do men. And, for some reason, friends and family seem to be more concerned about the widowed woman; whereas men are often thought to be able to captain the ship without outside help.

I am sure that widowed (and divorced) women and men

alike feel this social isolation—they feel the loneliness of being left out of their former circle of married friends. It is then that loneliness, self-doubt, and self-recrimination become the webs the mind can weave to keep one *in* the status quo, for in grief, as well as in normal times, one tends to fight change. I was strangely comfortable in the throes of my grief. The luxury of self-pity or self-guilt can become a means by which one puts off the responsibility of living and facing reality.

Somewhere in this mental quagmire of self-indulgence, I found the strength to fight back. It may have been something that was said to me. It may have been something I had read. Perhaps it was the thought that this wasn't what Beth would have wanted for me. Something caused me to reach—to reach out and grab hold of life and love. My happiness, health, and peace of mind were at stake. The first step toward a brighter future was in making up my mind to establish a new social life for myself. It was time to put aside such thoughts as: Is it too soon to go out? What will people think? It was time to accept the fact that I was a single person.

I made the decision to start dating again—the decision was not made easily. But I knew that the only way to escape this loneliness was through my own initiative. I knew I didn't want to live alone the rest of my life. In ten years or so, my children would be gone, and what would that leave me? Ten years without the love and companionship of a wife. That was not for me.

Once I had decided to establish a new social life, I still wasn't sure how to begin. My first step was to join a group for widowed persons called Widows and Widowers. This group gave me an opportunity to meet other widowed men and women and to enjoy the social life provided, such as dinners and dances at local nightclubs, theater parties, cookouts, bowling-team activities, discussion groups in private homes, and monthly social meetings. I had received several invitations to attend these meetings, and one night I just decided, this was it. It's a matter of starting a new life.

I felt like a stranger in town at first; I felt clumsy and uncomfortable. But it got easier. After all, most of us had become quite out of practice in this business of dating. My first date occurred only three months after Beth died. For some reason, I did not attempt again to establish a new social life for myself until another year had gone by.

I cannot speak for anyone but myself as to why a widower begins to think of women, dating, and remarriage. Like most men I know, my primary reason was the need for companionship—the warmth and comfort two people can offer each other. The void caused by a wife's death is a terrible emptiness. The gnawing grief brings on both emotional and physical pain. As time passes, part of the pain is healed. But the loneliness still exists, and one needs to seek some adult companionship. The need to regain a comfortable place in society, to satisfy emotional and sexual needs, to find a medium in which normalcy is all inclusive sends the widower back into the world of the paired.

Commentary

THE WIDOWER'S REENTRANCE
INTO PAIRED SOCIETY

What is meant by the "state of normalcy?" Bill found that
for him *normalcy* meant getting back into the paired
world. He and I have both experienced isolation from our
married friends—the fifth-wheel syndrome—as have almost
all formerly married persons. Brad, for example, a middle-
aged businessman, told me, "What amazed me most after
my wife died was the way people have stayed away or refrained from contacting me after the funeral. It was almost
as if I lived in a strange town. I guess people don't know
how to act or what to say. We were both active in social
affairs—my wife and I. We had lots of friends, but everything was done as couples. I get feedback from friends'
asking other people about me and wondering how I am
getting along. But very few, even several months after
my wife died, make it a point to visit, contact, or call me.
I know they like me and are concerned. I know they loved
my wife. We were known as the ideal couple and were included in more things than we actually wanted to be."

I don't think that our former friends are aware that
they are avoiding contact with us. As Bill said, "We remind them of the inevitability of death." Given the
taboo on the subject of death that exists in our society,
it really is not surprising that people want to avoid us. It

is almost as though by their ignoring death, it won't happen to them.

The widowed person is often at a loss to understand his friends' hesitancy and awkwardness toward him. George, a recently widowed young man, commented, "I think the only answer is death education to prepare people for their own death and to help them understand what it will mean when someone they love dies. Why should I have to add to my grief the burden of my friends' inability to deal with death? But I do. I try to act natural, you know, brave, as if nothing has happened. If only my friends could openly express their sorrow to me and let me express my feelings to them. It would help, too, if they could think of me as a normal person with the same need for companionship with them as before my wife died—even, perhaps, more so. I am thankful that many of my friends do."

The awkwardness that people feel toward the widowed is not one-sided. George is finding that it is very difficult for him to go alone to social events, even in his neighborhood among old friends. "My loss becomes so apparent to me when I am with married friends—how can it help but remind my friends of my loss? It's no use to pretend that I am not a reminder—rather let's believe that life goes on and it must," he exclaimed.

Other reasons for the isolation of the widowed exist. Adult society thinks in terms of couples. When a hostess is arranging a dinner party, the symmetry of her table setting would be askew if guests numbered five instead of six! And, furthermore, it has been the experience of Bill, and many other widowers, that husbands do not really appreciate having that extra man around. Women may, but not the men! A solution, of course, would be to have an extra lady, but for some reason it is simpler to invite married couples to a party given by married folk.

Ours is a couple-oriented society. It is also a family-oriented society, and a whole family means one with a mother *and* a father. It is sad that individuals must suffer the fifth-wheel syndrome. But equally unfortunate is the fact that *whole families* tend to ignore families with only one parent. Bruce, a father of three young children, angrily tole me, "I feel that my children are missing a very normal part of their life, namely, meeting other people in social situations. I want us to be invited to homes where a mother is present, but this is not happening. In fact, I have noticed that the friends my thirteen-year-old son is making in his first year of high school are largely from single-parent homes. The isolation from the married couple circuit is very real indeed."

Not only is this a paired society, but no clear-cut traditions or customs have been developed on how to behave toward the formerly married. A widower is perceived differently by different people. Many persons look at him as the debonair, man-about-town—a threat to other men. Married women may see him as someone who is dying to make a pass at them. My widowed friend, Tom, for example, tells of one of his experiences as a bachelor father: "I remember one day I was hanging sheets on the line, and I began chit-chatting with a neighbor lady. After a few minutes, I invited her over for a cup of coffee. She looked at me as though I had struck her, and she turned and practically ran into her house. Really, my only intention was to have a conversation with her. This is something that bothers widowers—living in a community where women don't know how to react to a formerly married man. I could talk to the men working in their yards on weekends, but most people just don't know how to take a widower."

Others see widowers as men half-crazy for sex. Bert, a widower in his seventies, remembers the remarks passed his way: "What do you do now to take care of yourself— or do you get so every woman looks good to you?" He goes on to say, "And some women, too, get pretty aggressive. These women aren't ashamed to let you know they would like to spend time with you in your bedroom. Maybe some men pursue this stuff; I don't know. I did not go for it. Sex without love isn't much."

While most widowed persons despair of their social isolation from married friends, not all widowers have that problem. Bert found that his close friends still remained close after his wife died and he remarried. He told me, "They have always done what they could for me, those friends of ours. Of course, at my age, many of them are dead, but I never felt left out by my married friends. This didn't stop me from feeling all alone though."

Other men claim that they have been pursued constantly, particularly by divorced and widowed women. Tom told me that just two weeks after his wife died, an acquaintance began bringing over desserts for his family's dinner. She made a pest of herself, and he finally told her he couldn't accept her kindnesses any longer. He commented, "And then there was the young gal who began inviting the whole family over for dinner. She was interested in me, but I was not—just two months after my wife's death. If women think they are the only ones who get propositions, they are very wrong!"

The widower, as well as the widow, has great adjustments to make in his life when his wife dies. Regardless of how friends and family react to him as a single man, he must find his own way into a new life. As George said to me, "I do believe that keeping busy soon after the death of my wife helped take the edge off my grief. I think old friends have their circle, and the sooner one develops a new set of friends the better. If not, one will feel everyone is against him when old friends prefer to associate with married friends and start leaving him out of their plans."

What can a widower do to escape his aloneness both emotionally and socially? Bill expressed the feelings of many widowers when he said that a very significant problem is the lack of adult relationship in which to communicate ideas and feelings. The need for companionship appears to be the most urgent need of widowers. As Tom told me, "I think that one of the biggest problems is not having someone to discuss feelings with, someone who can understand and relate with you without feeling that sex or remarriage is the goal for either."

Widowers generally seem to find it very difficult to begin a social life again. As Bill has said, "Widowers need to be contacted and helped if necessary by groups of formerly married persons." Some men, however, do not care to join social groups. They do not want or feel the need for a new social life. Other men do depend upon organized groups to provide them with a social life and an opportunity to meet new friends. Some find new friends through their work. Others turn to match-making friends and relatives for dates. However a widower gets back into the business of living again, the important thing is for him to get started.

Chapter 6

DATING AGAIN

A widower can find comfort, solace, and love within his family after his wife's death. He may fill his days with his job and his evenings with his family. But when it is time to go to bed, when it is time to be alone, the feeling of emptiness, nothingness, and barren despair overwhelms and drains him. Physically and emotionally empty, he falls into a restless sleep, which is unable to restore him.

It was this void that placed me on the path of seeking companionship. My search did not have to end in marriage. A lasting relationship with a close friend, male or female—someone who just would listen—would suffice. To be one of two adults involved in adult conversation would fill my need to be heard, to put into words the thoughts of and desires for myself and my family. Only through conversation with another adult could I look ahead with the proper perspective.

The give-and-take of ideas with another who is not emotionally involved can be a great help to a widower. It is extremely supportive for him to know he is not alone—that he has someone with whom he can have an exchange of ideas, someone who cares and wants to remove some of the stress from daily living. His fear of making a rash decision can be relieved by the action of talking it out. And companionship can have an extra bonus. In the proc-

ess of finding someone to *listen,* the widower might very
well find that the companion is pleasant to be with and
that mutual likes and dislikes exist. He might also find that
the listening is mutual, and each is giving equally to the
companionship.

When I first started to date, I found casual dating very
pleasant, as it provided me with an opportunity to have
adult conversation. Perhaps just being able to hear my own
voice speak the words I had been thinking, not really expecting any particular answer from my date, was what I
wanted most.

Dating was done primarily on my own. Most of my
relatives knew me well enough not to arrange dates for me.
They knew I would reject any of this matchmaking business. I probably would have reacted with resentment—con-
sidering it an invasion of my privacy. My grief was private;
I considered my social life private also. So I had to do
something about arranging my own social life.

Twenty years, more or less, had passed since I had had
to ask for a date. I picked up the phone, full of confidence, dialed a number, and the phone rang. She answered,
and suddenly my mouth felt full of cotton. I heard myself
stammering and muttering, and when I hung up, I had a
date. Why, I didn't really know. I was soaking wet with
perspiration—that smooth-talking, debonair man-about-
town is a bumbling, stumbling eighteen-year-old!

When going out by myself to a movie or to a meeting of
some kind, I had been telling my children, "I'll be back in
a little while." Now for some reason I suddenly went into
great detail letting them know, "I've got a date; my date is
Louise; we are going to a movie; and I'll probably be home
late!"

The night came for my date; I was ready early. Dressed

up all the way—sport jacket, shirt, tie, matching slacks, shined shoes. The car had been washed and I had kept the windows open all afternoon to get rid of the stale cigar smoke. The gas tank was full. Nothing was out of place. I was ready to roll!

I drove past her house hoping she didn't know my car, for I was early. I drove out of sight, parked, and waited for time to pass. I let my mind drift back to my first real date. Time sped by, and suddenly I was snapped out of my reverie. I glanced at my watch. I was late.

When the door opened and the lady stood before me, I was almost speechless, not because of her charm and beauty but because there I was with my mouth feeling full of cotton again. We were in my car driving to the theater when I found myself smiling, then chuckling to myself. She asked, "What's so funny?" and I told her all that had happened since my call. She nodded understandingly, for I was her first date in the three years since her husband died!

The evening then became pleasant and relaxed. We talked freely with one another. After we said good night, I noticed a slight bounce in my walk back to the car.

It didn't hurt a bit! In fact it was fun! Happier times were ahead. My head was back on straight. My thoughts were clear, and I felt more confident. I had resolved my inner conflicts, overcome much of my anger, and I was ready to take on the world again. Through the stumbling, bumbling stage of dating, I found myself enjoying my food more; dinner was no longer something to gulp down. I once again enjoyed eating dinner with someone besides myself. Some men will avoid places where they formerly went with their wives; they find new places. But I enjoy going to the same places I enjoyed with my wife. For my date, the happy, comfortable surroundings were new. For me, the pleasant, familiar surroundings now included my new date, and a whole new perspective developed because she was with me.

I now felt confident about dating again. I felt *single* again. I could enjoy dating. This time around I was in a better financial condition. I knew such things as the best places to eat, the best theaters to attend. I had had time to learn these things.

Some widowers fear the weekend. I had no fear of empty weekends, for when I could not arrange a date, I still had my family who also needed my attention. In fact, when I had frequent dates, I began to worry that I was ignoring my children. When that happened, my social life became a happy combination of both—my date and my children. I often invited my date to accompany me on an outing with my children—a visit to my parents, a Sunday dinner in our favorite restaurant. I thought it was good to involve my children in my dating to a limited extent, particularly when I became involved with the woman who was to become my wife. It was good for them to get to know each other as much as possible before marriage.

In establishing a new relationship with a woman, some widowers seem to feel a sense of guilt, as though they are cheating on their dead spouse. I have never had this problem. Perhaps this was because I knew Beth would want me to live a full life again, or because I had that long period of time during my wife's illness to adjust to the reality that I was going to be without a wife. Still, I would reach out at night to touch her, and she would be gone. I needed to touch someone.

I have been asked by people how long I think a widower should wait before he starts dating. This is a personal thing. One's personal needs and desires have to be met. If one accepts that traditional year, then one suffers through that year. If one is at ease with himself and with the person he is with, any time is all right to begin dating again. Whenever, the important thing is that one gets back on the road to being single again.

Man is a gregarious animal who requires someone to love, to want, to need, and, in turn, it is necessary for him to be needed. I believe the above statement covers most of the needs that companionship can satisfy. A widower needn't ask *Why?* when he chooses a companion; instead, he should ask *Why not?* Who he chooses is not really too important if he is true to himself and does not try to find another first wife. It's important to remember that he, at this time, is not the same man who married years ago. He cannot go back and obtain what is lost. Reality must dictate; the time is now.

By the time I reached the point of wanting to go out steadily with one woman, I had made up my mind that I wasn't looking for a replacement for Beth. First of all, I was twenty-five years older now than I was when I began dating my first wife. I was not the same person. I wanted to start again with someone new, to develop our own little world. I was looking for someone to talk to, someone who would be compassionate, sympathetic, someone to whom I could pour out my experiences and feelings at the end of the day—I was looking for companionship. I also found love, which is what makes life worth living.

Commentary

THE WIDOWER'S RETURN TO LIFE—
TO LOVE, ROMANCE, AND SEX

Bill speaks for most formerly married men when he says
that the number one reason a man starts to date and return
to the coupled world is a need for companionship—someone just to talk with, to have dinner with, to fill the void
brought about by the aloneness of being without a wife. In
talking with many widowers, I find that their advice generally is: "Go out dancing, relate, be yourself, and be
friendly. The sooner you decide to date, the better. Be
sure to date a variety of women. It's a matter of starting
a new life."

Whether a widower waits three months or a year after
his wife dies to begin casual dating, it is often difficult
to take that first plunge. "You feel clumsy and out of
practice" is a typical comment. For some, casual dating is
initially very pleasant; others find it very difficult. To a
great extent, success with dating depends upon one's
attitude.

Rick, for example, felt that life was over for him when
his wife of twenty-four years died. He told me, "I loved
my wife dearly and believed that I was incapable of finding anyone else I would want to marry. While I realized
that there would be value in finding someone to date, I
wasn't certain what was considered acceptable. I found a

copy of Amy Vanderbilt's book on what she considered *proper* form, and learned that it was considered appropriate to begin dating three months following the death of a spouse. To most men, I am certain my concern seems needless, but I had no desire to respond in any way that would not reflect good taste.

"I suppose I thought that I might marry *someday.* Most men have the capacity for loving more than one wife. This is an obvious fact that I didn't fully comprehend when I was living through those terrible days of loneliness.

"Abraham Lincoln once said that people are going to find just about as much happiness in life as they make up their minds they're going to have. There are people everywhere who need love. I must admit that my own response to my wife's death was not a good one. Instead of being grateful for the joy we had had together and looking ahead I kept looking back, creating for myself the most devastating psychological climate one could imagine. I am so grateful that someone found me and suggested that we spend a great life together."

Each person defines his situation according to his own personal needs and feelings. Like Rick, many widowers find casual dating difficult because they initially try to recapture the same deep feelings with the same type of person as their first wife.

Andy, a widower in his forties, had different problems. He told me, "At my age and with five young children, it was very difficult for me to find dating partners. Not only did I have babysitting problems, but I found that women shy away from entanglements with men who have young children. Also, I hesitated to date because I really didn't know how or where to begin or how my children would react."

Phil's dating situation was affected by his move to a new city shortly after his wife died. He had great difficulty getting acquainted with people. "I had no dates that I set up myself that first year. A couple I got to know arranged a few dates for me which didn't turn out. I remember on one date the gal took her poodle along!" commented Phil. "When I finally did begin to date," he continued, "I found it a very different pattern than going out with my wife. Dating doesn't compare with marriage, but I found the relations meaningful and, in some cases, quite deep. I started out by dating *safe* dates because I did not intend to re-marry at that time. So I would date either confirmed bachelor ladies or somebody whose religious or educational background would cause me never to marry. And I did have fun as a forty-year-old bachelor. My early dating, though, was primarily a special-event function. I would take my dates to a dance or a movie or to a party with friends."

Jake, at age forty-seven, found casual dating very easy. He told me, "I was widowed less than three months when I was invited to a party by some matchmaking friends, and I was dating in general soon after. I joined an organization for formerly married persons. I am a fun-loving person, so it did not take me long to find dating partners. Another thing, I never did feel that there is a once-in-a-lifetime romance. I always thought I could have been happily married to a different woman, even though I loved my wife and felt very lucky to have been married to her. She loved me, and during her long period of illness, she made it clear to me that she wanted me to find happiness with another woman and not wait too long. If a woman loved her husband, she would want him to be happy again; if she didn't, then what is the difference what you do?"

Andy mentioned that children posed a problem in finding women to date. Louis, at seventy-seven, found that children inhibited his dating, too, but in a different way. He told me: "My two daughters were married with families themselves when my wife died, and yet they seemed very resentful at the thought of their father even thinking about women and dating. They would tell me I was too old, or I should wait a while. But at seventy-seven, I didn't have much time. If I was going to spend two or three years looking for a woman, I might as well forget it.

"At first I handled my loneliness by spending my time in a tavern a few blocks from home. Because I knew those people and because they were good to me, I was there quite a bit. Then I would go home, putter around, look things over, and then, feeling *to hell with it,* I would go back to the tavern for a few more drinks. My drinking began to worry my girls more than the idea of my dating. But still, when I first started to date a woman I had known for many years, their resentment began to show. Nothing developed from my first attempt at dating, but had the girls not said anything, I might have continued dating her. There was another thing that caused me to hold back with this woman. She had several young children still at home, and I was already a grandfather with no appetite for becoming a stepfather to young children.

"I had plenty of money to spend and was very well known in our community, and lots of widows let it be known that they would like a date. But I wanted to find a woman who would become my wife—no more casual dating for me. I wasn't worried about what other people thought about how long I should wait to get married again. I was lonesome and depressed without someone to share my life. My idea was that if a man thinks dating will help ease his pain, he can move along very rapidly toward marriage. Just so he understands that other women can be just as desirable and loving and understanding as his wife had been. I wasn't going to worry about what my girls thought either. They are good girls and have good husbands, and they shouldn't worry about letting loose of the closeness we had. I have my life to lead, and they have theirs.

"Friends can be a wonderful help in finding a woman who might become your wife. They know you pretty well, and they have your welfare in mind. One Friday night, a couple that my wife and I used to chum with invited me to the country club for a fish fry. Once we got there, my friends pointed out a lady to me whom I had known for several years, but I did not know she was widowed too. They told me to go over and talk to her, and that started our courtship. I called her for a date, and we just seemed to get along well. She was happy, and we both liked to have good times. I was lonesome, and then all of a sudden my life was filled with happiness again. No more trips to the tavern. Catherine kept me busy going to dinners, and she even got me started golfing. We just liked each other. She has patience and a wonderful sense of humor. It only took a few dates to know we liked each other. I didn't kiss her the first date; I waited until the second one. She thought I was such a gentleman, not kissing her on that first date! Life was good, and in just three weeks I knew I wanted her for my wife."

Louis moved rapidly from dating to thoughts of marriage. He felt the urgency of time due to his age. He had matchmaking friends interested in his finding another wife, and he reacted to this with appreciation rather than with indifference or resentment, as some men are apt to react. Neither Bill nor Louis experienced the *she cannot be replaced* feeling, which tends to inhibit men from dating and eventually finding themselves a wife. And, like Bill, this grand old gentleman had no guilt feelings about his desire for the companionship and love of another woman.

Several widowers have told me they feel as though they are cheating when they first begin to think of dating. Louis thinks there is no reason to feel this way: "My wife was no longer with me, and when I had reached the limits of my mourning, I knew very well I had to have female companionship. I began to think about the companionship part right after she died. I knew I would never survive alone. I don't think that a widower should think he is cheating on his wife when he starts dating again. The relationship with my wife was separate and something special, and will be cherished as such. But the relationship has ended, and it does not prevent my establishing another meaningful one."

Widowers begin dating to fill their desperate need for companionship. But this does not mean that sex is not important. As Bill said, "For a time after Beth's death, there was no need or desire for sex. I was drained physically and emotionally. But slowly this need returned." Often it is when the need for sexual relationship is felt that widowers develop deep, serious conflicts in their minds about their sexuality. It is one thing to date, but the desire for intimacy, for sexual release, is something else, and it is here that severe guilt feelings may arise, with serious consequences. For example, Norm, a forty-year-old widower, suffered impotency as a result of the guilt feelings he had. His wife had been ill for several years before she died, during which time she was unable to have sexual relations. Thus, long before his wife's death, Norm had sublimated his own sexual needs with the exception of occasionally masturbating. His wife accepted his need for sexual release in this manner, but after she died, he even felt guilty about masturbating and ceased for a while.

There seems to be good evidence that men who have strong guilt feelings run the risk of becoming impotent, as Norm did: "I'll never forget the shock of discovering I was impotent. It was three years after my wife's death before I attempted to have sexual intercourse, because I always felt so guilty about wanting sex. One evening while shopping I met a widow whom I had known for years. She invited me to her apartment for a drink. She was in as much need for sexual release as I was. We went to bed only to the embarrassment of us both. I could not get an erection. So tormented was I at the thought of being impotent that I wouldn't even consider dating for several months.

"I met a lovely woman at a party who, after a few dates, began to arouse sexual feelings in me. We would have beautiful evenings in each other's arms kissing and petting. But I could not bring myself to chance a failure in sexual intercourse. Finally my desire for her became so strong that I suggested we go away together for a weekend. What hopes I had. We registered as husband and wife. When we got settled in our room we both wanted to make love. We showered together, we caressed each other's bodies. I had her in complete abandonment, and then it happened. Again, I was impotent. I knew she loved me for she was understanding of my plight and tried to lessen my embarrassment. We joined in mutual masturbation to achieve a sexual release, something we continued to do.

"We wanted to marry. We wanted to go to bed with each other and have intercourse. How wise she was, being contented with caresses and masturbation, not attempting to force me into intercourse. We had a beautiful love life, realizing that sexual intercourse is only one form of making love. Finally one evening it happened. I was no longer impotent.

"After not having had a woman for so long, sex was indeed a joyous, fulfilling experience. Until our marriage a while later, we regularly had sexual relations, although periodically I would go through a brief period of impotency when a feeling of guilt would return."

It is important for a widower to realize that his emotions have a great deal of control over his ability to function sexually. Guilt feelings very often keep a man from recognizing and fulfilling his sexual needs after he becomes a widower. In other words, men who have become inactive sexually may run the risk of becoming impotent; evidence is strong that a conscious attempt to sublimate sexual needs can result in impotency. I have become aware that many middle-aged men become impotent following the death of their wives. For most, this is temporary. It is a normal lack of the need and desire for sex felt by a man immediately after his wife's death. For others, impotency after several months of sexual inactivity may become a real threat. Joe, in this sense, was fortunate—a few months following his wife's death he received a phone call from a clinician and good friend inquiring how he was doing. Joe told me, "She asked me if I had found someone to sleep with, and I replied that I had not, nor did I wish to. She asked me if I had been masturbating, and I replied in all honesty that I had not—that I simply didn't have any sexual feelings and that I was having a difficult time. I was stunned when she asked me to promise her that I would masturbate before I went to sleep that night. In her very gentle way she explained to me that men who don't remain sexually active *may* become impotent. I have become very appreciative of her advice. I did masturbate whenever the need arose, and when I did meet a woman with whom I desired sex, whether masturbating helped or not, I was able to perform magnificently!"

Impotency is seen as a threat to a man who wants to remain sexually active. Long-term abstinence may make it difficult for a man to think in terms of becoming active sexually again. Medical science has a great deal of evidence to indicate that a man's sexual problems are primarily a matter of mind rather than physical disability. It is for this reason that I would suggest to a widower having difficulties with sex to seek counseling. Depression is a common cause of impotency. It is normal not to be able to function under this condition. However, since physical problems may be present, it is always a good idea first to have a physical examination. Once such problems are eliminated, as they will be in about ninety percent of the cases, one then might take a more realistic look at his expectations. For example, a man of sixty will have less stamina for sex than a man of thirty—his erection may not be as firm at sixty; but, even so, impotency is seldom a matter of aging. What a man may lose in plain stamina he may gain in qualities that make him a better lover, such as patience and durability.

Knowing that impotency is primarily a matter of mind and that, like all other parts of the body, the sexual parts function best with regular use, a widower should be encouraged to seek professional help if impotency continues beyond a reasonable length of time. A letter to the American Association of Sex Educators and Counselors (5010 Wisconsin Avenue, N.W., Suite 304, Washington, D.C., 20016) will provide a widower with the name of a certi-

fied sex therapist in his community. It is important to
know that almost all cases of impotency can be cured if
a man has the will to try.

We have discussed the widower's guilt feelings that arise
out of a sense of loyalty to his dead spouse. Religious
conflict can also cause guilt in a man's mind when his
thoughts turn to sex. Sam, for example, said, "I think it
was basically my moral-religious background that caused
me to have such a difficult time dealing with sex. In many
ways I felt there was nothing but a desert ahead, particularly in the area of sex. I had not been the kind of man
during my marriage who could bring myself to having
sexual intercourse with any woman other than my wife. I
have always been the kind of man who enjoyed fooling
around a bit in a flirtatious way—but nothing serious. Now
that I was without a wife, I found that I had problems
with sex. For instance, about six months after my wife had
died, I got involved in a relationship with a girl from my
office, and we had sexual intercourse a few times. This
relationship gave me sexual release, and we both knew
nothing serious would happen since neither of us had
thoughts of marriage. And yet, I didn't really enjoy this
sex experience. I felt so damn guilty (as though I had been
cheating on my wife) that I refrained from dating for
several months."

Without doubt, sexual frustration is one of the most
difficult problems faced by the widower. And again this
varies with personal needs. Ron, a young widower in his
twenties, found his need for sex compelling. He and his
wife had been very active sexually, and yet the deep love
he felt for his wife cause him to hold back thoughts of
remarriage. But he needed sexual release, and within a few
months found it through casual encounters. At first these

encounters were fun, satisfying, an ego trip, but he soon lost interest in them. Ron commented, "I realized I needed affection, a feeling of intimacy that I was not getting from these one-night stands. Sex with my wife meant being close, loving, and loved—a physical sharing. I wanted a relationship that would make me feel human and desirable. Something was missing in those casual encounters that I had had in my marriage—a feeling of exclusiveness, a one-and-only feeling."

Not being sure of what is expected in the area of sex also seems to trouble most widowers at some time or other. Joe comments: "I am basically shy with women, and when attracted to a woman, I simply can't say, 'Let's go to bed.' One evening I was with a great lady who was divorced. We talked about the problems of being alone. I said to her, 'How does a man go about asking a truly great lady like you to go to bed?' She responded, 'Honey, that's close enough!'

"It's not the words one uses that are the most important in extending an invitation to go to bed; it's the feeling that one conveys. No one whom I have asked to go to bed ever seemed offended. Yet, I was always afraid that I would offend someone. Had I known that many women are as fully sexual as I am, I would not have worried. When I was young, I got the idea that all sexual encounters should be confined to marriage. What a silly idea! Sex among loving friends is great."

This, of course, is Joe's personal opinion about sex before marriage. But it appears to me that he had a great deal of support for his point of view. Widowers have frequently said to me, "When two adults love each other and desire sex together, why wait until marriage? Surely we don't have to worry about virginity, and we aren't so inexperienced and irresponsible that we would be indiscreet or otherwise hurt the woman with whom we make love."

We have discussed the difficulty that many men have in finding dates, but this is not true for all widowers. Joe found it delightful that women made their availability known to him. He said, "Most men really are not offended if they receive an invitation to go to bed, and just as it is easy for a woman to decline, I have learned to say, 'I couldn't possibly do that, for if I did, I'm afraid you'd lose all respect for me!' I have yet to meet a woman who didn't laugh."

Probably the greatest help in coping with sexual frustration comes from the realization that most sane people don't expect widowed persons to quit being sexual at the death of their spouses. Understanding this, the widowed would not be so concerned about other people's opinions. Joe told me, "When people ask me now if I engaged in sexual intercourse during the time I was a widower, I say, 'Of course.' If people can't accept my response, they shouldn't ask. Although I am a very conservative person, I now find it pointless to lie. *Normal* people expect other normal people to respond sexually. Frankly, the people I wonder about are those who don't."

I agree with Joe that *"normal* people expect other normal people to respond sexually"—up to a certain age! When a person reaches the age of sixty or more, our society seems to consider him over the hill as far as sex is concerned. Louis, our elderly widower friend, said, "I know my daughters were plain embarrassed at the thought of their father still being interested in sex. They are young and in love with their husbands and can't understand how an old man like me can fall in love and be intimate with another woman. I don't think older people should remain single because they feel ashamed or too embarrassed to admit their sexual needs. They are afraid, too, that their family will make fun of them!

"I also think a lot of elderly people who get married or who are married think they can't or shouldn't have a sex life. They really miss out on a lot of life's pleasures, and it's much harder to get along together when you can't be intimate. I've always found that having sex makes me much easier to get along with. It's a special problem when one person craves sex, and the other spouse doesn't. I'm glad that I still have a good craving for sex myself. Keeps me young!"

It is a pity that so little is known about the sexual activity and attitudes of older people. There are many misconceptions about the role of sex in the lives of older people in our society, the greatest being that in the late stages of life sexual activity ceases.

We can blame these misunderstandings on the attitudes that people have about the elderly not needing sex and on society's failure to recognize the continuing sexual needs and desires of men and women as they grow older. Today, with the research we have showing that sexual activity need not cease with age, and, indeed, that our senior citizens do have sexual needs, it is unfair that such myths continue to exist. Given these false notions, it is not surprising that as people enter their sixties, they begin to think they *ought* to put sex aside even though they still have desires. Attitudes in our society that sex is not quite nice for older people, that sex is for the young, the notion that old is bad and young is good, all serve to make an older person feel ashamed of sexual activity or desires.

People should realize that aging is a gradual process, not something that happens when a person reaches a certain birthday. Aging involves a person's lessened physical vigor —but it is when a person begins to *feel* old, sometimes long before he has actually aged physiologically, that a person actually becomes old. As Louis has said, "Having sex together at any age is good—it makes you feel loved."

Since there is much to be gained from continued sexual activity into the later years, and since sexual intercourse is almost always possible, why is it that so many older people still continue to shrink from it? That is, why isn't more being done to educate the public, the doctors, the social workers, about the facts of aging? The popular belief that people past fifty years of age have little interest in sex would then no longer be the self-fulfilling prophecy it now is.

Sex is a vital part of any couple's marriage. Older couples should be told it is important that they understand and fill each other's sexual needs. They should be made to feel good about having sexual desires—not made to feel ashamed. Why not publicize that as a man grows older he has certain advantages over the younger man—his ejaculatory control is much greater; he is able to maintain erection for a considerably longer time, thus affording a woman much longer periods of enjoyment and opportunity to achieve orgasm. Even after prostatic surgery, if a man ceases his sexual activity, it is quite likely that he is looking for an excuse to end his sexual life because of feeling embarrassed or guilty about still wanting sex. Of course, if two people mutually agree that sex is no longer a necessary part of their marital happiness, then they should not be badgered into thinking they ought to have sexual relations.

The truth is that most men feel sex desires for as long as they live, and a goodly percentage of men are still

capable of sex into old age. Certainly the sexual respon-
siveness of the male does lessen as he ages, but I believe
that the greatest cause of decreased response is due to the
belief that sex is wrong rather than to any physical problems.

There are several other factors responsible for the lack
of sexual activity in later life. Some couples, after many
years of marriage, begin to take each other for granted and
become bored and disinterested in their marital relationship. Edward, a seventy-eight-year-old remarried widower,
expressed surprise at his renewed sexual vitality: "My first
wife and I just lost interest in sex. Hadn't had any for
quite a few years. After she died, I began going out with
other women and discovered that I still had the desire and
the ability. I think that the newness of a relationship,
when one begins dating again, has a lot to do with bringing
back that old spark. I'm like a romantic eighteen-year-old,
and I intend this time to keep the interest in love and sex
alive in my second marriage."

George, at sixty, told me quite a different story: "I
became so worried about what I would do about my lack
of economic security as I neared retirement that I didn't
even have sex on my mind. Most of the time, I would
come home from work too tired, physically and mentally,
to even want to try. I got in the habit of drinking myself
to sleep, and it seems that alcohol and getting an erection
don't go together. Now that my wife is dead, I'm afraid
to get involved with a woman for fear she might expect
sex, and I wouldn't be able to do anything about it."

There is no doubt that age, coupled with worry about
finances, or boredom, fatigue, or overindulgence in food
and drink can all have negative effects on a man's ability
to function sexually. But I cannot emphasize enough that

fear of failure is probably the most important reason the aging male withdraws from sexual activity. The notion that older men have no sexuality, when accepted by them, is very likely to lead to self-doubts and impotency. Remarriage for the elderly widower can provide the benefits of renewed and continued sexual activity if the couple realizes that their desire for sex is normal, too. I must add that if a widower is suffering from impotency, he can be trained out of it by adequate counseling.

Most widowers hope that dating will ultimately lead to love and marriage. Ron told me, "Sex was very important to me, but it is still only an outward expression of an inner feeling. Sex is most fulfilling when it is shared with someone you love." In other words, one's emotions may be the deciding factor, not only to whether one dates and remarries but also to the extent one can be sexually stimulated and satisfied.

Many men, because of guilt mixed with feelings of loyalty, cannot separate themselves emotionally from their deceased wife. These widowers who believe there is no replacement for their one-and-only love may find happiness in their life as a formerly married. But for the others, the important thing is to feel free to love, to have a sexual relationship, and to be as committed to another person as one would like to be. Friendship, affection, and love give meaning to people's lives and can lessen that terrible loneliness that affects all who have lost a loved person.

Chapter 7

THOUGHTS OF REMARRIAGE

Will I remarry? *No. No* is the easy answer.

No can mean that a man doesn't want to be hurt again. This attitude probably is, at first, the main reason a widower gives not to remarry. The loss created by a wife's death is so great that it, in most cases, divides him in two. Loyalty to his dead spouse and to his live family, together with recognition of his own need for living, rips him apart. Death is readily accepted; that it has happened to him is not.

No can mean that a man feels he is capable of raising his family alone. A man may decide, however, that additional help, possibly in the form of a wife, is needed. But he should not marry *only* to get help raising the children. "To thine own self be true"—that was my motto. I did not delude myself into believing that help was needed for the children. The help needed was for me. Love for a woman should be the motivating factor for remarriage, not children's needs.

The needs of the widower with children are great. The pressure of their care placed on him by society, family, and friends is a heavy burden that weighs on him when he needs no additional problems. But today, in ever increasing numbers, widowers are proving they can very successfully raise a family alone. It would be good if the widower,

111

supported by this fact, took a hard look at his reasoning which states he must remarry to provide a mother for his children. I find no fault in this type of decision, for it is because of his love for his children that it's made. But once again, "To thine own self be true." Happiness for me was equally as important as happiness for my children. If marriage for the convenience of my children was my only motive, I would have been trading a life of personal unhappiness in exchange for the children's happiness. In the final analysis, children in this kind of situation will be as unhappy as their father and his new wife. Other reasons for thinking of remarriage must prevail.

The cliché "different strokes for different folks" is true. Many reasons and feelings start the thought of remarriage. Usually the first thoughts are rejected. I was appalled at the fact I could be so unfaithful. I drove the thought from my conscious mind. It worked for a while, and I was back to the world I had been existing in. It wasn't a good world, but it had replaced my coupled world. Even though I was alone, I had become comfortable. These thoughts of remarriage were threatening the status quo; I resisted.

I thought many thoughts and preferred to stay with those with which I was most comfortable. The shroud of my grief, guilt, and fear was a façade between the world of today and me. I even wallowed in my own self-pity, but it was mine.

The mind is capable of doing many things. At times I could successfully shut off all thoughts of marriage. And when I did think about marriage, I told myself that I could never again find the kind of happiness I previously had. Yet, the death of my spouse had set me free, and I knew in my heart that I should feel no guilt. I thought of marriage, today, yesterday, tomorrow. In my mind, I was back in the world of the couples; I was back on familiar ground. Why not?

When I finally decided that the woman I was dating was the one with whom I would like to spend the rest of my life, questions still arose in my mind: wasn't my first love unique, a once-in-a-lifetime experience?—my first marriage was so perfect, could anything else replace it? I put aside these thoughts. I realized that Beth wasn't the only woman I was capable of loving. This didn't mean that I loved her less because I had found someone new to love and to spend the rest of my life with.

Why did I remarry? Because I was in love, and this answer is the only true and wonderful reason. Although love defies description, I link it to a tightly woven cable. Its strength is based on the whole, not on the individual strands. The strands are hope, respect, honor, trust, desire, understanding, and listening, among countless others. These strands are held tightly together by the bond of love. As one whole cable, the widower gives love to the woman he wishes to marry and finds love for himself. The woman should not be considered a surrogate mother for his family; anything less than real love for her will return him nothing but unhappiness.

If one starts with love as a base, one can adjust or re-adjust to conquer one's specific reason or objection against remarriage. The mutual respect, admiration, and regard for the loved person is the broad base to build on. If true friendship is included, one is ahead of the game. Once I had accepted the fact that I was in love and that my feelings for a woman were stirring again, I found that any objection I had against remarriage disappeared. I was a single man in love again!

When I accepted the fact that I did want to remarry, I

was not looking for any particular kind of woman. I just knew that Jane was the woman I wanted for my wife. She had all of the abilities, all the physical and personality attributes I wanted in a woman. She was interested in me and obviously I was interested in her. We had many things in common, a mutual respect and love for each other. And so we were happily married.

Commentary

THE CHOICE TO REMARRY OR REMAIN SINGLE

As Bill has said, there is no single path leading out of the dissolution of a marriage and into a new life. Dissolution of a marriage has a different meaning for each individual. Each widower may find a different path in healing his wounds and returning to a reasonably happy life again.

For some widowers, the path to happiness is remarriage. Other widowers enjoy their newly found freedom and intend to maintain it for a variety of reasons. A widower without children, for example, may be very mobile and want to remain free to come and go as he pleases with no marital strings attached. Martin was sixty-five when his wife died. He was still in good health, had a comfortable retirement pension, and the yen to travel. He enjoys the companionship of women and frequently will take with him on his travels a younger widow whom he has been dating. They both enjoy dancing, golf, tennis, and boating, as well as the travel. Martin told me, "At my age, loneliness is the main thing to avoid. I keep active and remain in contact with my family and friends to avoid being lonely, and I do a damn good job of it. You know, the first few months after my wife died, I nearly died of loneliness. A really aggressive woman almost snagged me. Men in my situation are an easy target when they are grieving because they don't have their heads on straight. My advice is to just

115

sit tight and get into the business of living as soon as possible. I have had the best that marriage can give me, and so I don't intend to marry again. I'm going to be buried beside my Bertha," he concluded.

Elderly widowers such as Martin may be content with happy memories. On the other hand, a widower may have had such a hellish first marriage that it would take much convincing for him to risk marriage again.

Once an elderly widower gets through the stage of severe grief and loneliness, societal and family pressures support his remaining single. He isn't expected to have a sex drive, and even if he did, chances are he has learned to sublimate these feelings because "old men aren't supposed to feel this way." His children are grown and don't need a mother. In fact, often they would rather not have him remarry, for this would threaten their expected inheritance!

Some of the loneliness may be abated for the older man if he moves in with his children or into a retirement institution. Of course, this choice depends upon the kind of hospitality and care he receives. Churches and various social and government agencies provide many activities for the older man who seeks companionship. Free community meal service, parties, card clubs, and the like are also provided the elderly in many communities. An elderly widower who wants to remain single finds support for his decision in social acceptance and he is provided with opportunities to interact with other elderly singles.

On the other hand, the young man whose wife dies is pressured to remarry whether or not he has children. Society believes every young man *naturally* should want a wife, particularly if he has been widowed. He needs sex; he should become a father if he is not one already. If he is a father, his children must have a mother. Ron, for example, was a young man in his twenties, going places in the work world. He had a wife and three children, aged one month, two years, and four years. Then the phone call—his wife is dead, killed in an automobile accident.

Ron's situation was desperate. What help is there in our society for a man left with three babies? Little, if any. Ron, fortunately, had a mother who could stay with him temporarily. After a few months he was able to obtain live-in help. Child care and household needs were solved.

As time passed, Ron found there was much more to his desire to remarry than providing a mother for his babies. He wanted a wife with whom to share a loving, intimate relationship. Within the year after his wife died, he married a girl of twenty-two who had not been previously married.

Given the social pressures to remarry along with their own personal needs, most young widowers do remarry. However, for the young widower who chooses to remain single, there are sources that will support him in his choice. The woman's liberation movement has encouraged people to resist the push toward marriage. Sex outside of marriage has become more acceptable and more readily available. Bachelorhood has even become glamorized. Men share apartments, which provides needed companionship and friendship. Ken, for example, a twenty-five-year-old widower, was severely criticized by his family because he decided not to remarry immediately. He told me, "My marriage was not all that blissful. My wife and I had many fights about spending money and relationships with relatives and friends. Now I enjoy making decisions on my own instead of jointly. I like the flexibility of my daily schedule. I can spend money and go places spontaneously without any feeling of guilt. I enjoy the diversity

of contacts with people. I enjoy the sexual freedom I have.
Many possibilities are there. My wife was the only girl I
went with, so now, if and when I do remarry, I will have a
better idea of what kind of a woman is best for me."

Some widowers with children also remain unmarried.
Ed, for example, still had a ten-year-old daughter at home
when his wife died. He told me, "My daughter needs me,
and I don't think she would adjust to my marrying again.
She and I are very close; our relationship satisfies my need
for love and companionship. We are real pals, and I am
content with our family life just the way it is. My son is
in college; he adds to my fulfillment. I am a man of financial means, so social life is no problem. I have joined some
singles groups and have met other single men and women
through my work. My sexual needs are met through a
relationship with a divorced lady who also has no desire
to remarry. She is a liberated professional woman married
to a highly successful career." Ed concluded, "I don't
even feel single yet; I feel like a family man. My first marriage was very satisfying, and after five years, I still don't
feel the need for another marriage. Maybe some day . . ."

Bill has suggested reasons for a widower's saying "No"
to remarriage. Perhaps Ed does not want to risk again the
hurt he suffered when his wife died. Maybe he is waiting
until his children are grown and on their own. Perhaps his
needs are such that he will never emotionally get single
again and, thus, will remain unmarried. I agree with Bill
in that it is a matter of personal decision. I, for one,
know that happiness is possible, married or unmarried, if
one is willing to put forth the necessary effort.

Many considerations affect the choice to remarry or to
remain single. Doug, for example, told me, "I am in poor
financial straits, and within another year, I probably will

be out of a job as my employer goes in for more automation. How can I take on a new wife—no matter how badly I might like to be married?" Al had another reason for not remarrying. Health. Al has had a heart condition for the past twenty years, and after his wife died, he felt he had no right ever to expect another woman to marry him. He asks, "Can I have happiness again? No, I can't expect another woman to sacrifice her life to care for a sick man."

Remaining single is an alternative way of surviving after the death of one's wife. Remarriage is the other alternative. Many factors enter into the decision to marry or not. When a widower is twenty-seven, he will have different considerations than when he is sixty-five. A happy first marriage may turn him toward remarriage, while an unhappy first marriage may discourage him. If he is in a good economic situation, he may prefer the mobility of not being married rather than tying himself down again. Several children still living at home may motivate him to remarry quickly "for the sake of the children," or he may decide to postpone marriage until the children have grown up and left home.

Will he remarry? That depends on the widower's expectations for his future. When a widower remarries, his expectations are as great as when he married the first time. Perhaps the expectations are now even greater, for at this time the needs of family and self are greater. He has made all the mental adjustments necessary to marry again. He has hopes, emotional expectations, and looks forward to a beginning as well as to an end. This is the climax of his reentry into the coupled world, which he lost with the death of his wife. Once again he and his wife will be one and accepted as such. No longer will he be a fifth wheel. No longer will well-meaning friends arrange chance dates.

Once again his house will become a home. Once again there will be a feeling of warmth and love contained in those four walls. He knows that there will be problems because he has been down the road before. But as Bill said to me, "The first night I came home and knew that there was someone there who cared and loved me, I knew things were going to be better." The soon-to-remarry widower expects his mate to be someone who listens, who has an interest in his welfare, and who returns his love with honest feeling.

How soon will he remarry? That depends on his adjustment to being single again—to his feeling that his first wife is dead and he must make a new life for himself without her.

Chapter 8

STARTING ANEW

It was just about a year and a half after Beth died that I began dating Jane, and it wasn't long afterwards that we knew we wanted each other and realized that we could have a happy life together. We had a love for each other that encompassed friendship, mutual respect, admiration, and care.

When we made our decision to marry, each of our families was paramount in our thoughts. But we also knew we had ourselves to think about, and that if any difficulties did occur, time was on our side. My children are all old enough that in a few years they will be on their own. Jane's son and daughter are already married and on their own.

We made the decision to live in my home and to remodel it to include a private area for us—something I think is necessary when one brings a new wife into an already established family. The intimacy of two people in love and newly married need not be shared with children!

Marital responsibility to my new wife and to my children suddenly became compounded with the possibility of disagreements between them. Deciding where one's first responsibility lies is very difficult; it varies with the age of the children. If the children are young, they are more adaptable and can fit into the new situation; they adjust more readily to a new wife's way of doing things. However, my six children were older, ranging in age from twelve to twenty when I remarried. Their characters and their thought patterns were established. There was very little room for them to change or accept a new set of values, a new way of doing things.

All of my daughters are independent and outspoken and, of course, there have been disagreements between them and Jane. But once again, our commitment to each other has been strong enough to overcome the mental anguish brought about by children who always speak their minds and who have a great love for their own mother which causes them to still think of our home as *their* mother's home. At times it is impossible not to become emotional and forget logic. At this point, in fairness to the memories they have of their mother, as well as in response to Jane's right to take her place as my wife in our home, I walk a very narrow line. I don't choose to be a mediator. By and large, Jane and I believe that she and my daughters should be able to work out their disagreements among themselves. I do not want to have to decide who is right and who is wrong.

While disagreements are certain to occur in any family, we agreed that any differences or conflicts would be talked out. Some conflicts may never be resolved, but when the children are all gone from our home, Jane and I will still have each other because our commitment has been first to our marriage.

We are happy that the personal, sexual, and spiritual relationships between us are exactly what we want them to be. In all areas of our marriage, we have reached a common ground of understanding by being honest, direct, and open with each other. We have come to terms with our drives and our needs so that we satisfy each other's wishes, desires, and hopes.

Throughout our book, many references have been made to my deceased wife. The love I had for her and the life we had together is over. Only memories remain. They are but the path behind me. In retrospect, the beginning steps of that life were light, fanciful, and hurried. They slowed in maturity and stopped in death.

Now, writing for myself and Jane, I find the steps once again have become light and fanciful. We hope the wisdom of maturity will allow us the happiness that comes with love, respect, and the desire to fill each other's needs— to love together, to laugh together, and, if need be, to cry together.

Commentary

REMARRIAGE—ITS PROBLEMS, ITS POSSIBILITIES

Bill has reminded us of the many thoughts that go through a widower's mind as he contemplates remarriage. He told us how he at first hid behind the façade of grief, guilt, and fear of the unknown future. But then it happened. He fell in love again, and found that it can be even more wonderful the second time around because he was more prepared, more knowledgeable about what makes a happy marriage. Remarriage for the widower, then, holds out the same potential for happiness as does marriage the first time. However, development of this potential in a second marriage varies according to the personalities involved and the situation in which the couples finds itself. A young couple with very young children will have special problems, as will a middle-aged couple with teenage children or an elderly couple with no children living at home.

Probably widowers with children form the largest group, so it seems appropriate to talk about them first. While many factors come into their decision to remarry, concern for their children is paramount in their minds. However, it is not until a widower is satisfied that his children seem established in their new motherless situation that he should begin to think seriously of marriage.

Henry describes his adjustment to remarriage and the

problems he and his new wife shared when they put together a new family circle of her three children (a daughter, age four; a son, age eight; and a son, age ten) and his three daughters (ages eight, fourteen, and eighteen).

"About six years after the death of my first wife, I remarried. I didn't have any single reason for getting married again. Instead, the reasons were multiple: companionship, love, sex, and sharing life. This combination of needs caused me to think of remarriage.

"It wasn't that I was feeling a need for a new mother for my kids, although it is interesting that my first wife's cousin wrote to us shortly after my wife's death suggesting that I should marry for the sake of the children. (I think most of us widowers resent the notion that no man can rear his children. He can be a very adequate parent.) When I did decide to get married, I talked it over with my daughters. I did not ask their permission. Of the women I dated, the one I married was the one they liked the best. I received no obvious negative reaction to my remarriage from them prior to the wedding. However, following the marriage, there were some negative reactions.

"It was the little things that caused the problems right in the beginning. I had run the household for several years, and I had certain ways of doing things. My three daughters and I moved into the new home that my present wife and I had purchased three weeks prior to our marriage. At that point, some of my furniture, as well as some of hers, was moved in. We left the living room largely unfurnished because we wanted that to be something both families did together. One of the biggest difficulties arose over the kitchen. When my daughters and I moved in, we set up the kitchen very much as we had our previous kitchen. And then my fiancée would bring in some of her things, and she would rearrange the cupboards. As soon as she left, my daughters would arrange things as before."

This type of conflict between stepparents and step-children almost always develops. In first marriages, women feel no challenge in assuming their position as head of the household in terms of housekeeping routines and child rearing. Husbands traditionally are the final authority when it comes to serious discipline problems with the children and the spending of money. Most children are born into an established family circle with roles already defined. Then during widowhood, the single parent assumes sole responsibility for fulfilling the needs of the family.

Remarriage is different. It plunges two newly marrieds into two already established family routines. Henry's older girls were not only very self-reliant, but they had run the household completely for their father for six years. They cooked, kept the house, picked up, and looked after the younger one. Could they now be expected to relinquish their authority over their younger sister, and to give up making decisions regarding housekeeping and cooking chores? What about their sense of loyalty to their departed mother for whom they were still grieving and for whom they felt a deep love? What about the possessiveness and protectiveness they felt for their father? Didn't they feel a sense of rejection at the thought that he didn't need them so much anymore? How did they feel when they saw their old and familiar furniture and fixtures being moved out of their house to make room for new furniture to match the new decorator scheme? These are all things about which children are bound to have strong feelings, and Henry's wife, Betty, was wise enough to understand this. But understanding did not make it any easier for her to take her place beside Henry in her proper role as co-head of the family.

The girls could not accept Betty's authority, for it had not been clearly defined for them. Prior to his remarriage, Henry, in trying to placate his daughters, established a position of equality between Betty and his girls. He did this to assure them that they were no less loved or valued because he was taking another wife. This, of course, could not work. If all were equal, then Betty had no more authority than anyone else. She found herself in an impossible situation. Many times she was told, "You don't have any more rights than we do, so you can't tell us what to do around here." At first Betty tried gently to get across to them that it was her prerogative as their father's wife to assume household responsibilities. She even communicated her wishes to the children through the oldest girl so as not to upset the chain of command. She resisted the urge to take over the cooking; however, since she was working full-time, who did the cooking was not an urgent problem. But their resistance to allowing Betty any authority held until finally she realized that she either had to "knock heads together," as her mother-in-law suggested, or allow the children to keep the reins and not let it bother her. At first, Betty chose the latter, and the older girls assumed she was afraid of them.

Betty seriously thought of leaving many times. Fortunately, she exploded instead. When Henry became fully aware of what was going on in his family, he became more assertive in establishing Betty's position of authority as his wife, whether the children liked it or not. Now the pressure is off. The children are beginning to accept the fact that Betty is around to stay. Some of them are voluntarily picking up the house, cleaning their bathroom, doing up snack dishes, and when they don't, Henry reminds his daughters of what is expected of them. He may even do the chores himself rather than cause a discussion.

Once lines of authority in the family were clearly defined, confusion lessened. This is true in any family. Parents must be sure of who they are. In our conversation with Betty and Henry, she said, "I can be more relaxed in relating to my husband's children now that I have established my own identity with respect to them. I hope that, as they establish their own homes, they will come to appreciate my situation. I don't expect to become anything other than a friend to my husband's daughters, but being grandmother to all of their children would be nice."

In discussing his position in the family, Henry agreed with many other widowers as he said, "The most difficult role I have found myself in has been that of being in the middle. Loyalty to my natural children, wanting to be fair to my stepchildren, and loyalty to my second wife rip me apart. Only after my two older daughters had married did they actually begin to understand the need my wife had for acceptance as "head lady." Only one daughter has looked upon my wife as a mother. Amy has a daughter of her own now, and this Christmas, when she and her husband came home for the holidays, she related to my wife as a mother—not as her mother, but as one mother to another. Understanding and empathy were present. In the beginning of our marriage, however, our children clearly did not accept us. She is not our mother! He is not our father!"

Confusion, hostility, rebellion, refusal to accept the authority of the stepparent, all almost always become

significant problems in second marriages. Henry and
Betty's situation was no different. Henry continued, "Even
after several years, I am reminded that I am not the *real*
father by my wife's now seventeen-year-old son. This boy
frequently remarks, 'You didn't ask me if you could marry
my mother.' Finally, I told him, 'No, I didn't ask you if it
was all right if I married your mother. I had no intention
of doing so because I was marrying her; I was not marrying you. I appreciate your concern, but as long as you are
of the age where you are living at home, I am the father
and will continue to make certain decisions regarding your
behavior. When you become of age, more decisions will be
yours to make. But until that time, your mother and I
are the bosses around here.' "

I told Henry that I believed it is important for a couple
getting married to realize that under normal circumstances
they will have more time alone than they will have with
the children, regardless of the ages of the children at the
time of the marriage. This, of course, does not apply to
children born of the new union. Usually, after a maximum
of six to eight years of marriage, the couple will be alone
and may have another fifteen or twenty years together.

Henry said, "Yes, I agree. Neither of us means to sacrifice ourselves for the children's happiness. We have told
the children that the two of us are the husband-wife,
the mother-father; they are the children. 'These things you
will do. These things you will not do.' Now the kids may
blame the other parent for the things they don't like,
but then the natural parent has to say that both parents
agree on the rules and limits set. The kids may get upset
or angry, but kids get put-out with their natural parents.
Look how many children move out of their natural parents' home and how often the natural parents feel a sense

of loss, and, perhaps, guilt. I know this happens, but still I have felt a deeply personal sense of guilt and even failure over everything that does not work out as desired.

"At first I reacted badly to my sense of failure with my stepchildren. I even began to stay away from home and to drink too much. Now I tell myself that I will do the best I can with the children, and, if things don't always work out as they should, that's tough, but it's just a fact of life. And since I have made that decision, the situation has been much better, and I have discovered that I am getting more support from my wife than I did before. When I say 'This is it, I am not going to budge,' I do get her support and the children's respect. Of course, I don't do this all the time."

This is one of the main problems in remarriage. The newly married couple takes too much personal affront when they can't resolve a family conflict. How can the new stepparent take even a six- or eight-year-old child who has grown up in one kind of a family environment, who has developed basic values, who has gone through the serious hurts and joys of childhood, and change him to meet new specifications? Both parents must do the best possible for the children, but neither can take the *total* responsibility for what happens in the new family.

If there are children involved when a man remarries, he must realize right from the beginning, as did Henry "Yes, we love our children, and we will do the best we can for them, but the primary thing is our relationship with each other."

A husband and wife must build up very strong support for one another, and this is going to hurt, for it may be necessary to change family patterns that have been followed before. Such simple things as TV viewing, meal-

times, and types of food served may have to change, and
this change can cause difficulty. But the couple must be
willing to face the hostility of their children and be able
to say, "Look, this is the new situation, not unlike the
changes one has to make when moving into an entirely
new culture."

Suddenly, adjustments by all are necessary, but the two
adults, themselves, have to be willing to face the hostility
of those whom they have depended upon. Henry told me,
"I depended on Mary, Amy, and Janie for love. Now I
still want them to love me, but after I was married, the
situation changed—I didn't need them in the same way. To
them this was a rejection, and you have to be willing to
face this hostility. I think, if you know that this is not
just your problem but one that all remarried couples
have when children are involved, the situation becomes
easier to accept."

Widowers and divorced men have similar problems with
remarriage, but the widower's problem is special, for in
most cases the attitudes toward the deceased mother are
very favorable. In the case of a divorce, the feelings may be
positive on the surface, but underneath there is hostility
which the children recognize, so the new wife coming in
may be a sort of substitute for the previous mother. The
attitudes toward her may be mixed; whereas, following
death, the attitudes toward a deceased mother are often
idealized out of proportion. The new wife is an interloper. "And not only do the children idealize their
mother," said Henry, "but many times after my new
marriage, I found myself idealizing my former wife. This
is probably normal, although it is unfair to the second
wife."

Henry continued, "A widower remarries for many of

the same reasons he did the first time, such as for companionship and love and the desire to share our lives with another person; yet we spend all of our time trying to make it with the kids. I think we should keep our mind on the purposes of our remarriage: because I love this gal, I want to live with her, I want to go to bed with her, I want to have fun with her, I want to do things with her. I didn't marry her to get a housekeeper or a mother for my children. We say these things, and yet when there are children involved, we forget all of these reasons for marrying our second wife because we are bombarded from all sides about caring for the kids. 'Don't let them get hurt by this new union!' And so we go overboard in our loyalty to our own children."

Most widowers say they suffer from split loyalties: loyalty to the new wife and loyalty to their children. They are caught in the middle and forced, unfairly, to play the role of mediator. Sometimes a widower becomes so frustrated by the power struggle between his wife and his children or between himself and her children that he wants to walk out or just give up and let them fight it out.

As a consequence of split loyalties, the husband and wife can become extremely defensive and paranoid. A wife may distort the slightest criticism. For example, if he says my kid is too fat, or has sloppy manners, or should make his bed in the morning, I may think he is saying I am a bad parent. We often take our spouse's criticism of our children as a personal rejection. "He is picking on my child, he doesn't really love me." No one likes to be told that a situation he thinks to be progressing smoothly is not. Look how defensive some of us get when a teacher criticizes our child. And yet, we know the teacher is try-

ing to help. It must be realized that this is the spirit in
which the spouse is relating to the children.

Henry exlaimed, "Lordy, I know this, and yet why
should I get so uptight at times? I knew when I married
her that she had some different values, different ways of
doing things, but I wouldn't have married her if I hadn't
also known that she had many good qualities. She is going
to try to instill in all our children, hers and mine, her outlook on the way things ought to be in our family. Certainly, I am going to try to reach out in the same way to
the children by teaching them or at least encouraging them
to accept certain of my values, too. But my values, my
ways of doing things, may not be important to her, and
then when she rejects what I am trying to get across to the
children, I feel rejected and this rejection sets up negative
feelings between me and her children. It can also cause
negative feelings between my wife and her children, for
if she supports me, she feels she is being disloyal to them.

"We should not allow these kinds of difficulties to deter
us from remarriage. But we should be aware of the kinds
of things that can happen when children are involved."

Remarriage is a different ball game from first marriage.
As a matter of fact, our culture really has no clear-cut
definition of remarriage. Even the traditional marriage
ceremony seems inappropriate. When two people with
children marry, it seems appropriate to include the children in the ceremony. Henry tells about his marriage
ceremony. "When the minister pronounced us husband
and wife, he also pronounced us the mother and the
father of a new set of brothers and sisters. Our two families were united. However, we knew that whether they
learned to like one another or not, the relationship would
develop and must be accepted as the best that can happen,

given the situation and personalities involved. That her children may not like my children should never be allowed to diminish the happiness that is possible in remarriage."

Joining two families is never simple or easy. Henry decided within a year after his remarriage to adopt Betty's three children as a means of establishing more family togetherness. Henry tells of this experience: "At this time, we had need for counseling. Children certainly should be brought into the discussions and given information about what adoption means, for as we found out, it can be a trying experience. We had a grotesque experience with an insensitive judge. The first question he asked me was, 'Do you love your wife's children as much as you do yours?' I wanted to say, 'Of course not, you dumb nut.' We had been married less than a year, so how could I? But I told him yes, because I had been warned by our lawyer not to cross this judge. Then our eleven-year-old son was brought into the procedure. The judge asked him if he wanted me to be his father, and if he wanted to have my name. Then he leaned over the bench and said to the boy, 'Do you realize this means he can punish you and discipline you and do anything he wants to for your welfare?' That was the sum total of the adoption proceedings. It was all a very negative experience for us.

"After nine years, I think the three younger children may think of themselves as being brothers and sisters. The older ones still view each other as people they know quite well, but they don't think of themselves as brothers and sisters. It is very unrealistic to dwell on molding two families into one. You just have to live together as best you can and let develop what will." Many parents feel they are failing if they can't or don't work things out so that stepchildren learn to love one another. It is a mistake to be overconcerned about this. Love between children can't be manufactured.

It is important to be realistic about relationships in re-marriages—not only within the immediate family, but with other relatives as well. Henry said, "When I remarried, my first wife's family had a very positive feeling toward my new wife because they had felt that I should remarry. When we went to visit them, she was very well received, but they couldn't help but show preference for my natural children; they had known them since they were babies, and the other children were new to them. The same thing happened with my second wife's parents. They showed preference to their natural grandchildren. They never forgot to send them birthday gifts, but seldom do they remember the birthdays of my three natural children. At first I found myself being hurt by this seeming neglect, but I shouldn't feel this way." Henry is correct. It is unrealistic to expect grandparents, for example, to feel the same way toward children brought into the family through remarriage as they do toward their natural grand-children.

In remarriage, where children are involved, the couple must understand that they need a stronger sense of com-mitment to each other, a stronger recognition of the need to work to make their marriage happy. Long-standing ways of doing things that developed during the first marriage are added to the normal problems of marriage, and de-mands of children who are not theirs, split loyalties, are a part of a second marriage. There must be such a strong feeling of love and determination to make a marriage work that these built-in conflicts will not destroy the marriage.

Where children are concerned, one must realize that, in the heart and mind of a child, a stepparent can never replace the real parent. The case of Ali, a widow with no young children of her own who married a widower with several children, clearly illustrates this. After three years of marriage, Ali still feels a sense of frustration over her inability to establish the kind of relationship with her stepchildren she had hoped to have.

She told me, "After three years, I have not been accepted even as another friend in the household. I am Ali, someone their father married. If someone should mistakenly refer to me as 'mother,' the fifteen-year-old winces, and I am certain she wants to correct the false assumption. Even though I think she likes me, she has asked her father to tell me not to be so nice to her because she doesn't want another mother. It almost seems as though her sense of loyalty to a mother she dearly loved causes her to have a sense of guilt at being too warm or close in a relationship with her father's new wife."

When I told Ali it might help if in some way her role in the family were more clearly defined, she replied, "They don't know who I am even yet. For example, when they bring someone into the house and introductions are in order, they will stammer a bit and say, 'Well, this is Ali'— or 'She is my father's wife.' Even the eldest daughter, age twenty, with whom I have had very few problems, told me recently that she still didn't know how to introduce me. They don't want to acknowledge any form of motherhood, not even that of stepmother. If my husband is present, he will immediately ease the introductions by saying that I am his wife. The older girls particularly seem to find it difficult even to acknowledge this, although they have told me they appreciate the happiness their father has with me."

We agreed in our conversation that the age of children

makes a big difference in their ability to adjust to a new spouse in the home. If children are very young, they can begin to identify one another in the family circle through names. A young child may find it very simple to call the new husband or wife "Dad" or "Mom." When children are older, there has to be an identity established through relationships. In other words, if the children could be encouraged to introduce Ali as "my father's wife; they were married three years ago," Ali would be put in the role of wife. But according to Ali, she still feels unrecognized by her husband's children—almost as though she were being thought of as an interloper. I advised Ali to accept her situation—to tell herself that this is the way it is and to go on from there. She can't legislate feelings, and she should not feel herself a failure because she has not been accepted as she would like to be, despite her many efforts.

When asked if the children show signs of recognition such as borrowing money from her and asking for favors, Ali replied that, with the exception of a few cases when there was absolutely no one else to turn to, only the youngest girl ever asked her for anything. She also told me that they resisted being asked to do anything by her. She has found that if their father asks them to do whatever she would like done (such as light household chores), they are much more willing to comply. Perhaps this is the only solution, given her family situation. It certainly would tend to lessen potential conflict. Ali says that she always feels as though she is walking on thin ice—never quite knowing what the reaction of the children will be.

One possible solution to the "this is our real mother's house" attitude toward Ali might be for the family to move out of her husband's home where he had lived with his first wife. Ali, for example, thinks that she would have a better hand in the situation if they develop a new home together, free from the familiarity of the past.

"Whose house did you move into when you remarried?" is a question so frequently heard that it must be considered an important issue. Does it really make a difference whether the couple contemplating remarriage moves into his house, her house, or a house new to both of them?

Conversations with women who have remarried show that establishing a new family circle is simpler when the husband and his children move into the wife's home, rather than into his former home. This is her base, and stepchildren do not have the seniority claims such as Ali has had to deal with. Of course, in this situation the husband has a more difficult time in establishing his identity as joint head of the household, for his wife's children may consider him an intruder in *their* home. The natural father is still at home in the minds of the wife's children. Yet, the stepmother does have the more difficult role because she is more likely to be in constant, often day-long, contact with the children in the more personal aspects of family living, such as child care, meals, laundry, general household matters. Often, the father is not in close touch with the daily affairs of the household and is not so likely to run into problems with the children as is the wife. Either way, one group of children are insiders, one outsiders.

Consensus among remarried persons with children seems to be that, where possible, it is best for all concerned to move into a home that is new to both families. If this is a joint operation, it can bring the family closer together. At least, the question of seniority is eliminated—which is not to say that other potential problems are.

When children are involved in a second marriage, many

adjustments must be made if a reasonable amount of peace and happiness is to be achieved in the family circle. But whatever the adjustments, it is important that a couple put themselves and their marriage *first*. And the children must be aware that their parents' marital needs will be of first concern. Husband and wife must support each other and must be willing to risk the hurt and hostility from their own children when they stand by each other.

If the husband and wife do not behave in a mature manner in dealing with their children, the children will develop an out-of-focus picture of their family situation. It is difficult to remain patient, to resist giving in to a strong desire to fight hostility with hostility. But parenting requires this kind of self-control. When we allow anger to influence our thoughts and behavior toward our children, we lose control of the relationship, and the child wins the battle. If we allow an atmosphere of anger and hostility to encompass our family environment, we can be sure that the children will respond to us in anger and resentment.

Some parents react to their inability to reach their children by becoming very submissive and by allowing the children to make all the decisions. This, too, leads to aggressiveness, disobedience, and greater feelings of insecurity and anxiety in the children, and they might even begin to think that their parents don't really care about them. This can lead to a "who cares?" attitude in which a child loses the desire to make any effort to get along in the new family circle.

While I have said that it is vital that we parents establish clear-cut lines of authority, I do not mean to say that a dictatorship is recommended. When making decisions, parents should always try to put themselves in their children's places in order to understand what this new situation means to them. When parents understand their children's needs, they will be better able to make the right choice in decisions affecting the whole family. Following Henry's example, children who are old enough to make decisions should be brought into family discussion. They should be given a democratic voice in decisions that affect them. They should always be offered reasonable explanations for the changes (new rules, new ways of doing things) in family living that are taking place. If these things are done, children will be more likely to accept the changes in a reasonable time. How long acceptance of the changes may take depends on many things: ages of the children, personalities of the children, acceptance of the remarriage, acceptance of the stepparent, the desire and ability of the remarried couple to achieve harmony in the home, and, very importantly, how well the parents have been able to establish two-way communication between themselves and the children.

Mark and Mary, for example, have one of the happiest remarriages we know of, and it involves a total of nine children. The key to their successful family union was that they worked to establish open communication. Of course, time helped, too. If given a fair chance, children do come around. Mary's teenage son at first refused to accept Mark. The first time a father/son banquet at school came along, he refused even to ask Mark to attend. The second time, he accepted Mark's offer. This year he enthusiastically invited Mark and said he would like to share Mark at the banquet with another boy who didn't have a father to go with. "A sense of humor is essential," Mark says. "The things children do to let you know they are resisting the new order of things are often very funny if seen in the right light." We should learn to laugh at ourselves so that our children can laugh with us, not at us.

Bill and I have learned the importance of having reasonable expectations. I think many of us expect more from our children than is appropriate for their level of maturity. A thirteen-year-old should not be expected to behave as an eighteen-year-old! And we should try to be as realistic about ourselves, too. We are not perfect either. We can admit to our own mistakes without a sense of failure. We must do the best we can, always remembering that it is our marriage relationship which is most important to us. If we are happy together, our home will reflect our happiness. It will be a warm place for living.

Remarriage, of course, involves much more than dealing with relationships between children and the husband and wife. Henry speaks of other areas of adjustments he has had to contend with: "I know there were periods early in my marriage when I became so uptight and frustrated at things that were going wrong that I would fantasize about how perfect things were in my first marriage. One night I broke down in bed and cried—it was on the anniversary of my first wife's death. I found this good in one respect, that Betty then realized that I had not completely forgotten my first wife, that I did have some deep feelings for her. She helped me work through some of my feelings. She would say such things as, 'Karen and I are alike in this respect, we are different in this way,' and this worked out very well for us."

Idealization of the deceased mate can and usually does create problems in remarriage. This is particularly true when the new spouse suffers because of unrealistic comparison. It is absolutely necessary that widowed persons contemplating remarriage first reconcile their feelings for their second spouse in relation to their first. In remarriage, when the second wife is compared unfavorably with the first, she may feel that she is not satisfying her new husband. He may say, "We always liked our roast beef well done." She may interpret this as, "He doesn't think I can cook as well as she." On the other hand, if a widower makes a comparison favorable to his new wife, he may feel a sense of personal conflict, of disloyalty to his first wife: "If I really loved her, how can I think my new wife is so beautiful, or maybe I didn't really love my wife the first time as I should have." These kinds of comparisons can contribute to feelings of guilt, and it is probably best to try to avoid them. Two persons who are secure in their love will not usually be haunted by such thoughts. But for the person who has doubts about himself, emotional problems may ensue.

I reminded Henry that a widower must realize when he remarries that he has had a certain number of years invested in his first marriage and that he can't wipe that out, nor should he. He can't blank out his previous marriage, but he should put it aside. He should let go of things that could hold him back in his new marriage. Some things may have served well in a previous relationship, but their usefulness is over. One must be willing to change. "Yes," Henry agreed, "you must change—for the person you are now marrying has different strengths and weaknesses than the other person had. I may have had to act one way with Karen, but now I have to act another way with Betty."

Remarriage is a learning experience—even more than the first marriage. A remarriage is complicated by the fact that it is influenced by both one's previous single experience and his marriage experience. We are all amateurs in our second marriages, almost as much as we were in our first. There are serious problems and little problems, joys and tears, in most marriages. As we have seen, one of the most difficult problems is acclimation of children into a new family situation. Leonard, my widowed friend with three very young children, had no problems with this, however. His second wife, Sarah, was a loving person, and she had a deep maternal feeling toward his children. As young as they were, Sarah had no problem becoming "Mommy" to them. Their problems were with religion and in-laws.

Leonard's first wife was Catholic, and, understandably, her parents wanted their grandchildren to be brought up in that religious faith. Leonard was not Catholic, and neither was Sarah. He had never made any promises to his first wife about their children's religious upbringing, nor had she asked him for any. Now he intended to bring up all of his children, and those he and Sarah hoped to have, in his and Sarah's faith. His former in-laws could not accept this. They kept putting pressure on both of them, even suggesting that Leonard and Sarah give up the children. While Leonard wanted to preserve the relationship between his children and their grandparents, it became more and more difficult. Leonard told me, "I didn't want to subject my second wife to a continual hassle with my former in-laws. When an opportunity to take a new job in another city came along, we decided to move."

True, remarriages have special problems, but it is possible to solve or contain them just as we do in first marriages. Religion can be a source of conflict in any marriage if a husband and wife have different religious faiths and values or are unreasonable in their demands. An interfaith marriage did not seem to cause difficulty between Leonard and his first wife. But religious conflict between him and his former in-laws became a very real threat to family adjustments within his new family circle. Leonard said, "Religion won't be a problem in our marriage because we discussed it honestly and openly prior to our marriage."

The expansion of family relations is another issue that arises in most marriages, but it is potentially more problematic in second marriages. Not only does the newly married, widowed person have to adjust to new in-laws, but, where stepchildren are involved, it will probably be necessary for him to adjust to his new spouse's former in-laws. The children may want, and have a right, to maintain as close a relationship as previously existed with the relatives of the dead parent.

Of course, there are relatives, and then there are relatives! Some are likable, and others can never be considered even as a friend. The closeness of a relationship will depend on many things, particularly on how much both sides desire to maintain it. In cases such as Leonard's, where children are very young, no enduring relationship has had time to develop. But I believe that older children should be encouraged to continue their relationships with their dead parent's family, as do Bill's and my children.

I have been very fortunate—Bill's former in-laws have been very loving and supportive of me. I encourage their efforts to preserve the memory of the girls' mother. Ali was not so lucky, for her husband's former in-laws tried to poison her stepchildren's minds against her in their efforts to idealize the memory of their daughter. This did no one any good—it hurt the children rather than helped them. Most in-law problems begin with the mother-in-law and daughter-in-law, so it can be a double problem for a widower. He must add his second wife's relatives along with his first wife's relatives to his list of potential problems. In-law problems, however, can be avoided if the widower provides strong support for his wife. In addition, the remarried couple can use good judgment in avoiding conflicts over trivial things and particularly over things they cannot change. The couple can also realize that in-laws, present and past, can be very helpful. They can provide emotional support, love, understanding, and advice out of their own experience.

Major issues such as children, in-laws, and religion are important to consider, but Tom reminds us that little things can also cause problems. "I don't want to underestimate the little things that can creep into a remarriage to cause trouble," he said. "For example, where I put my toothbrush in the bathroom is a part of my mode of operating. Now granted, if I am going on a camping trip or something else for a brief period, I am willing to make some changes, but I feel that I have a right to certain traditional, familiar ways of doing things, and my wife feels the same way. So you have to realize that these habits do clash. People can trace back to their first marriages and find similar differences. But now you have made one switch—from being single to marriage, then back from marriage to non-marriage, and now you are changing back to married life again, and this is not a thing that becomes easier just because you have repeated yourself.

"As a widower entering remarriage I had many patterns to change—spending money, eating, entertainment, all sorts of things. The period during which I was living alone with the kids was a time of developing new ways without my wife; for example, we even developed certain menus to suit our new style of living. A very little thing, but still a part of it even after nine years, is our taste for preparing wieners. I like them cut up and cooked in baked beans or just boiled in barbecue sauce. My wife likes to grill them, which we all call 'burned,' before she covers them with barbecue sauce. I find myself running into the kitchen to fix the wieners before she can get a chance to burn them. Well, this is just one of those little things that can create problems."

It is the little things that can grow into big problems. These little trifles can become tremendous problems unless they are talked out and resolved in some way. For example, Jim told me about how angry he would get because his wife persisted in leaving the cover off the tube of toothpaste. He found a simple solution—"his" and "her" tubes. A sense of humor goes a long way in handling these troublesome little things.

Both a wife and a husband going into remarriage have established ways of doing things, which require compromise on the part of each. Perhaps the widower has a more difficult time in adjusting to change because of the sort of mystique that has been created about him as a single man, be he divorced or widowed, and which he himself has accepted. You know how it goes, "Man is master of his fate, captain of his soul, and I am going to run the show." And many women encourage that attitude. What happens when this widower marries a woman who has not identified with the traditional notion of male superiority? She may at times have given the impression that she views man in the traditional manner, but when her behavior belies this, it may come as quite a shock to the widower.

Another factor that affects a widower's adjustment to remarriage is how valuable and how pleasant or unpleasant the period of singleness was beforehand. If, prior to remarriage, the widower had been completely miserable, he would make a poor marital partner. Obviously the same situation also would exist if the widower had felt that his singleness was absolutely wonderful. There is a type of autonomy that a widower has enjoyed that can be painful to give up. When he remarries, he must give up some of this autonomy in building a new relationship with his wife and between their two families.

I don't want to make remarriage sound all negative. But most of us know the positive things about marriage, and it is important to know some of the special problems of re-marriage beforehand so they can be better handled. The adjustments that must be made are a fact of remarriage. But even with the rough spots, remarriage can be very much worthwhile.

Remarriage has many advantages over first marriage. For one thing, most of us are more mature, more aware of what it takes to make a marriage work, and thus, we are usually easier to live with the second time around. As Henry told me, "When I was married the first time, I had many of the very traditional expectations regarding the role of the wife. Some of those were knocked out of me by my first wife. So from my own point of view I am much more mellow—and, very frankly, I think my present wife is probably easier to live with than she was the first time around. Part of this is because of physiological and social maturing, but part of it also is because we are more aware of the really important things we can get from living as husband and wife. This is why I say remarriage has been a very positive experience for me, as it is for most of the people I know who have remarried. Most importantly, we must get things in perspective, and I go back to problems with children. Things will work out if we can say to ourselves, look, our kids will be around for x number of years, and we should have twice as much time, or more, to ourselves after they are grown and on their own. We should not let the ending days of our marriage become fouled up by these tensions and irritations that can be caused over children. The first few years of any marriage can be rough in terms of the need for adjustments to marital and family roles. But if these first years can be weathered, a beautiful marriage can be achieved."

We have talked at length about remarriage for the widower with children in his care. But what about the elderly widower whose children are grown and on their own? To answer this question, I asked Howard, a happy, healthy former widower, to tell us about his feelings and experience with remarriage.

Howard, in his eighties, and Marie, in her seventies, were both widowed before their marriage, she for six years, and he for two years. Their first comment to me was: "Remarriage has an outstanding advantage over the first time—experience. We have learned about what to do to bring ourselves happiness and what to do to avoid conflict." This couple is so obviously happy that their feelings about remarriage cannot help but be relevant to anyone who might be hesitating to remarry. "We feel sorry for some of our friends who feel embarrassed about wanting to marry again or for those who worry too much about whether their kids will like it. More and more we feel how fortunate we are to be healthy and happy and have the means that will allow us to live together and do the few things that we want to do. Things, that when we were younger, we didn't appreciate as much as we do now."

Howard believes that he would not have survived his recent illness if it had not been for the great desire to live that Marie's love and care gave to him. He said, "I've had quite a lot of sickness since we married. She's been through it all with me, and her cheerfulness and care have brought me back to good health. We're very active today, and people can't believe that I'm back on my feet, even better than I was before."

"And what's so nice, too, is that we are able to enjoy a happy sex life because we are so healthy and love one another," added Marie. As I have discussed earlier, it is very unfortunate that elderly people so often put aside their sexual needs because they think they have become too old for such things. Howard told me, "I know some fellows who would like sex, but their wives don't go for it anymore. If you can't have that affectionate feeling, you're really missing something. Sex goes on beyond the age that I expected and anticipated it to, but thank goodness Marie enjoys sex, too. There's no question about it. Two people together, no matter what their age, will know it when they feel affection for each other, and it's really great."

Howard and Marie recaptured the romance of youth when they met. He told me, "After our second date, when I kissed her, I knew she was *it.* That was about a year after my wife died. I called Marie, and we just seemed to get along well. I was lonesome—all of a sudden, I had been left alone. I had had a good life with my wife, and when she was killed all of a sudden, it was a terrible shock.

"I had been out that day fishing with some of the boys. I came home around six o'clock, and I can remember the beautiful sunset. When I drove in, she came out to greet me as she always did, 'Hurry up, Howard, and come in the house. I have a good dinner waiting for you.' So we ate our dinner, and then she brought out a big platter of molasses cookies. She knew how I loved those cookies. After we had our cookies and coffee, she told me she would like to go to the grocery. Well, on the way, some drunken man came behind us as I was turning in the driveway to the store—and that was it. When I woke up in the hospital four days later, she was buried. Nobody saw her body because she was blown up when the car exploded. I had been thrown from the car. I can't even tell you the anguish I felt when I came home to an empty house after several weeks in the hospital. My daughters stayed with me for a while, but eventually they had to go home to their families. Well, I felt as though life was no longer worth living."

Howard was unable to get over his loneliness and depression, and for a time, he sought solace in the bottle. It was not until he decided that he had to find a better way to live that he began to date, and shortly thereafter, he met Marie. From the widowers I have talked with, it seems that those who have had a happy, well-adjusted first marriage are very likely to find contentment through a loving relationship with a woman. Likewise, they are not likely to feel guilty when they turn to another woman for companionship and love. Howard said, "I can't understand why men should feel guilty about getting married again. If their first wife loved them, wouldn't she want them to be happy? I don't think I ever felt disloyal or guilty. But that is not to say that I don't think of her, even today. I can dream, and it all comes back the way we used to be, and when I wake up in the morning, it kind of shakes me a little. But, after all, I was married to this lovely lady for forty years, and that's quite a lot of living with one person; we were very close. Besides being a wonderful wife and

mother, we had our own business, and she was the book-
keeper—so we worked together almost all our lives."

When I asked Marie if it bothered her to have Howard
speak of his first wife, she laughed, saying, "Just about the
molasses cookies—that she could make them and his
daughters can and I never could learn to make them!" It
was clear that Marie did not suffer from any comparison,
as Howard demonstrated: "They each added much to my
life, and I know I wouldn't have wanted to miss out on
the wonderful life Marie and I are now having." Marie
added, "I didn't realize I was *not* happy until I met
Howard, and now I know how good remarriage can be.
I think a lot of people who are widowed kind of envy us
when they see how happy we are."

There are many reasons for the happiness this couple
has found. They obviously have a joyous outlook on life,
coupled with a sense of humor and the ability to communicate with each other. Marie assured me, "There's
one thing about Howard, if something is bothering him we
talk about it." Howard agreed: "I would say that being
able to talk about everything saves us from having any big
problems. That and having consideration for each other
and being fair. That's the main thing—and being open and
learning to give and take with each other." Marie continued, "And we can laugh together about things. Remember the anniversary card you went to town to get for me
and the card said, 'From the both of us.' You had just
picked up the first card you saw. We have fun. We have
both families together for holidays. I think Howard's
daughters and sons-in-law are as close to me as my own
sons."

In the early part of their marriage, Howard and Marie

had some problems with their children even though they were grown up and living on their own. There was the usual testing of the new wife by Howard's daughters. For example, when the daughters would come home, they were likely to rearrange things or say to Marie, "This is not the way we used to have things." To which she replied, "Maybe not, but this is the way it is going to be in *my* house." Following the couple's marriage, her twenty-year-old son had the feeling that his stepfather's home was not *home* to him. Marie recalled, "The first time he came to visit me after we were married, he didn't stay with us. Then the next time, he came and brought his suitcase just like he was really coming home, and, boy, did that make me feel good." "Now we all get along well," Howard exclaimed.

Being open and considerate in their dealings with each other's family is the primary reason that Howard and Marie were able to make the family adjustments that they did between themselves and their children. They are very happy about their family situation. As Howard said, "I can say that one reason we're getting along so beautifully is that both of my daughters have accepted Marie one-hundred percent. And her boys have been very nice to me. It's just a wonderful feeling all the way around. It has meant a lot to me to see how happy Marie is and how nice the girls are to her. We are accepted by both families, and that is the way it should be."

A subject which has not been brought up yet is the matter of inheritance. I have become aware that many elderly persons are persuaded by their children not to remarry because of their children's concern over property rights and so forth. "Selfishness, I call it," said Howard. "A person ought to be free to live his own life without interference from his children. What is done with property is also the parents' business until they die." Howard and Marie felt that it was best to sell her house in the city and move into his home, which is located in the country. Marie said, "I don't think I could be happier anywhere than I am here. I had some second thoughts about moving into his house—but I was the younger, and I thought it would be easier for me to adjust than for him. Of course, my boys thought it was a good idea—they like the idea of being out in the country to fish and hunt."

The two sets of children are satisfied that their inheritance rights are protected, and this has prevented the kind of bitterness and hostility that can grow between families when such things are not settled fairly. For example, Howard told me, "Before we were married, we talked to our lawyers and had an evaluation made of each one's possessions. What she had when we were married (savings, checking account, stocks and bonds) remain hers in her name, and what was mine will remain mine. Naturally, that division will continue even if one of us goes. Her folks will keep what she's got, and if there's anything left of mine, my folks will get that. In the meantime, we are going to enjoy our life and not worry about what is left. We share the daily expenses—even our wine and brandy. Our children tell us to enjoy our life and not to worry about leaving them anything. And with the taxes going sky high, maybe there won't be much left to worry about. But it's nice to know that I have everything arranged as far as dividing things between my daughters fairly and fixing it so that Marie won't have to worry about expenses if I die first. She can live in this house as long as she wants to. She doesn't have to worry much about the future. She also has two wonderful sons to take care of her if need be." Marie added, "My sons don't expect anything from my estate—just so Howard and I have everything we want."

By talking with Howard and Marie, as well as several other happily remarried elderly couples, I am convinced that remarriage is a far better solution to loneliness for an older widower than is living alone, with relatives, or in an institution for the aged. I must qualify this statement with the recognition that marriage at any age can fail without careful prior thought being given it, without feelings of companionship, affection, and love, without the willingness to make necessary concessions for the happiness of the other, and without primary commitment being given to each other as husband and wife. Any venture one undertakes involves risk, and so it is with remarriage. A young man may remarry and find that his wife cannot love his young children; this can be heartbreaking. A middle-aged man may remarry and falter under the burden of playing middle-man between his wife and his children. An elderly gentleman or lady may be more subject to illnesses and to an early death. Marie, for example, saw Howard through one heart attack and two operations. Yet they believe that the joy and blessings they have from being together in their later years far outweigh the risk of sadness and tears which will surely come to one or the other.

In retrospect, the death of a spouse truly loved is a traumatic experience under any circumstance. It is not, however, the end of life for those who mourn. Marriage together may have been of long or short duration, but in that span of time, love and respect for each other have had time to develop. As time passes, a mutual sense of purpose develops and grows in most marriages. All this does not die with the death of an individual, though grief may make everything seem lost.

If a deep relationship based on love and concern for

each other existed, the bereaved will find strength and purpose during the period of adjustment after the death of a spouse. The day-to-day activities do go on. Children must be cared for; they must be clothed and fed and loved. Household duties must be continued. The trauma that a man experiences when his wife dies and leaves him, often suddenly, with the full responsibility of a household is great. It is likely that he has had little or no preparation for assuming the day-to-day activities since typically it is the wife who has tended to the home and children. Now the surviving individual must address himself to the problems of living.

For some widowed persons, the period of adjustment is long; for others, it is short, depending upon the individual's needs and circumstances. Many find comfort in old friends, in new friends, in family. Those who have religion and hold to it throughout life have another source of comfort and strength. Many of our widowed friends have said they found the strength and will to go on from their religious faith—that their faith made it easier to accept the reality of death and the fact that they must carry on.

After a period of time, facing the activities of living life alone begins to take on new meaning. Strength gained from children, relatives, friends, religion, and from the realization that one is getting along alone gives one the impetus to venture forth to seek new activities, a new social life. It is a fact that many old friendships and associations of the past seem to drift away. This isolation from old friends has been referred to as the fifth-wheel syndrome, affecting men as well as women, and can only be alleviated by individual efforts to resume a social life. In time, new associations can become as important and meaningful as the old.

Breaking the hidden barrier that seems to hold one back

from asking for that first date or from accepting an invitation from a woman for dinner in her home is the first big step toward a new life. A widower may feel uneasy about making that first step. He may experience a feeling of guilt or a sense of disloyalty to his first wife which causes him to hesitate. Once the decision has been made, however, it becomes easier to begin new relationships. A widower may then find it helpful to become associated with a group of people in similar circumstances—widow or widower groups, single-parent groups, singles groups. Getting involved in school activities, political organizations, church functions, and the like also can provide new associations. Sharing mutual problems and developing new friends contribute greatly to creating a new life for oneself.

Once a widower begins to establish new social contacts, his mind may turn to thoughts of remarriage and he may begin to date with that in mind. The right woman for him is most likely to be a woman with whom he has shared interests. She is honest, has a sense of humor and optimism, and is a good listener. She is a person who understands that the past cannot be forgotten—that each partner will need to talk about the past, and she will be able to listen to these reflections without feeling a sense of comparison.

Having found this right person, a man will want to marry her to fulfill his greatest needs—companionship and love. A happy sexual life is also considered important. A widower is likely to believe that if he and his new wife have companionship and love and concern for each other's happiness, then sex will be handled to the mutual satisfaction of both. Remarriage can be that silver lining within the dark clouds of grief.

SELECTED BIBLIOGRAPHY

1. THE IMMEDIATE REACTIONS TO THE DEATH OF A LOVED ONE

Caine, Lynn, *Widow* (New York: William Morris and Company, Inc., 1974).

Glaser, B. G., and A. Strauss, *Time for Dying* (Chicago: Aldine Press, 1968).

Grollman, Earl A., *Concerning Death: A Practical Guide for the Living* (Boston: Beacon Press, 1974).

Kubler-Ross, Elisabeth, *On Death and Dying* (New York: The Macmillan Co., Inc., 1969).

Kubler-Ross, Elisabeth, *Death: The Final Stage of Growth* (Englewood Cliffs, N.J.: Prentice Hall, Inc., 1975).

Rynearson, E., "You are Standing at the Bedside of a Patient Dying," *CA*, May-June, vol. 9, no. 3 (1959), p. 85.

Saul, L. J., "Reactions of a Man to Natural Death," *Psychoanalytic Quarterly*, vol. 28 (1959), p. 383.

Schneidman, Edwin S., *Deaths of Man* (New York: Quadrangle, The New York Times Book Company, 1973).

Schneidman, Edwin S., *Death: Current Perspectives* (Palo Alto, Calif.: Mayfield Publishing Company, 1976).

Silverman, Phyllis R., *Helping Each Other in Widowhood* (New York: Health Sciences Publishing Corporation, 1974).

Shultz, Gladys Denny, *Widows Wise and Otherwise* (Philadelphia and New York: J. B. Lippincott Company, 1949).

Stein, Sarah B., *About Dying* (New York: Walker & Co., 1974).

Toynbee, Arnold, et al., *Man's Concern with Death* (New York: McGraw-Hill, 1969).

Vernon, Glenn M., *Sociology of Death: An Analysis of Death-Related Behavior* (New York: The Ronald Press Co., 1970).

Weisman, Avery D., *On Dying and Denying: A Psychiatric Study of Terminality* (New York: Behavioral Publications, Inc., 1972).

158   The Widower

2. ACCEPTANCE OF DEATH AND
RECOVERY FROM THE PAIN OF GRIEF

Bincer, Wanda L., "How to Cope with Loneliness," in *The Personal Problem Solver,* Charles Zastrow and Dae H. Chang, eds. (Englewood Cliffs, N.J.: Prentice-Hall, Inc., 1977).

Glick, Ira O., Robert S. Weiss, and C. Murray Parkes, *The First Year of Bereavement* (New York: John Wiley & Sons, 1974).

Greenwald, J., *Be the Person You Were Meant to Be* (New York: Dell, 1973).

Grollman, Earl A., *Living—When a Loved One Has Died* (Boston: Beacon Press, 1977).

Kastenbaum, Robert, and Ruth Aisenberg, *The Psychology of Death* (New York: Springer Publishing Company, 1972).

Leonard, Calista U., *Understanding and Preventing Suicide* (Springfield, Ill.: Charles C Thomas, Publisher, 1974).

LeShan, Eda, *What Makes Me Feel This Way?* (New York: The Macmillan Co., 1972).

Lester, Gene and David, *Suicide: The Gamble with Death* (Englewood Cliffs, N.J.: Prentice-Hall/Spectrum Books, 1972).

Parkes, C. M., B. Benjamin, and R. G. Fitzgerald, "Broken Heart: A Statistical Study of Increased Mortality Among Widowers," *British Medical Journal* (1969), 1:740.

Parkes, C. M., and R. J. Brown, "Health After Bereavement: A Controlled Study of Young Boston Widows and Widowers," *Psychosomatic Medicine* (1972), 34:449–461.

Silverman, Phyllis R., "The Widow-to-Widow Program: An Experiment in Preventive Intervention," *Mental Hygiene* (1969), 53:333–337.

Silverman, P. R., "Services for the Widowed," in *Social Work Practice* (New York: Columbia University Press, 1966), pp. 170–189.

Stein, Z., and M. W. Susser, "Widowhood and Mental Illness," *British Journal of Preventative and Social Medicine* (1969), 23:106.

Young, M., B. Benjamin, and C. Wallis, "Mortality of Widowers," *Lancet* (1963) 2:454.

Zim, Herbert S., and Sonia Bleeker, *Life and Death* (New York: William Morrow and Co., 1970).

Zastrow, Charles, "How to Handle Being Depressed," in *The Personal Problem Solver,* Charles Zastrow and Dae H. Chang, eds. (Englewood Cliffs, N.J.: Prentice-Hall, Inc., 1976), pp. 29–34.

3. HELPING A CHILD FACE THE REALITY
   OF DEATH AND COPE WITH GRIEF

(Asterisks indicate children's books that deal with some aspect of death and dying.)

Beckman, Gunnel, *Admission to the Feast* (19-year-old girl, dying of leukemia, writes a long letter to a friend in an attempt to stabilize her crumbling world), (New York: Holt, Rinehart and Winston, 1972).

Blank, J. P., "To Be Young and Know That Death Is Near: L. Helton's Esteogenic Sarcoman," *Reader's Digest,* (January 1972), 100:78–84.

*Blue, Rose, *Grandmother Didn't Wave Back* (New York: Franklin Watts, Inc., 1972).

Burgess, Jane K., "How to Adjust to the Death of a Parent, Close Relative, or Friend," in *The Personal Problem Solver,* Charles Zastrow and Dae H. Chang, eds. (Englewood Cliffs, N.J.: Prentice-Hall, Inc., 1976), pp. 54–82.

Cooper, R.M., J. G. Sobosan, and J. A. Phipps, "Facing Death," *Christian Century,* (February 21, 1973), 90:225–32.

"Death with Dignity: The Debate Goes On," *Science News,* (August 19, 1972), 102:118.

*Dobrin, Arnold, *Scat* (New York: Four Winds Press, 1971).

Forbes, C. A., "Death: No More Taboos," *Christianity Today,* (May 26, 1972), 16:31–2.

Gallagher, T., and T. Morris, "Can Death Ever Be Merciful: Pros and Cons," *Good Housekeeping* (January 1972), 1974:90.

Green, Betty R., and Donald P. Irish, eds., *Death Education: Preparation for Living* (Cambridge, Mass.: Schenkman Publishing Co., 1971).

Grollman, Earl A., ed., *Explaining Death to Children* (Boston: Beacon Press, 1967).

*Grollman, Earl A., *Talking About Death* (Boston: Beacon Press, 1976).

Hoffman, J. W., "When a Loved One Is Dying," *Today's Health* (February, 1972), 50:40–3.

Jury, Mark, "The Nobility in Gramp's Decision to Die" (photo essay), *Today's Health* (January 1975), p. 18.

Kastenbaum, Robert, and Ruth Aisenberg. *The Psychology of Death* (New York: Springer Pub. Co., 1972).

Kubler-Ross, Elisabeth, *On Death and Dying* (New York: The Macmillan Co., Inc., 1969).

Kubler-Ross, Elisabeth, *Death: The Final Stage of Growth* (Englewood Cliffs, N.J.: Prentice-Hall, Inc., 1975).

Kubler-Ross, Elisabeth, "Facing Up to Death," *Today's Education* (January 1972), 61: 30–2.

*L'Engle, Madeleine, *Meet The Austins* (New York: The Vanguard Press, Inc., 1960).

LeShan, Eda, *What Makes Me Feel This Way?* (New York: The Macmillan Co., 1972).

Lewis, Oscar, *A Death in the Sanchez Family* (New York: Random House, 1969).

*Miles, Miska, *Annie and the Old One* (Boston: Little, Brown and Co., 1971).

*Orgel, Doris, *The Mulberry Music* (New York: Harper and Row, 1971).

Pincus, Lilly, *Death and the Family* (New York: Random House, 1974).

*Rawlings, Marjorie, *The Yearling* (New York: Charles Scribner's Sons, 1939).

*Rock, Gail, *The House Without a Christmas Tree* (New York: Alfred A. Knopf, 1974).

Schneidman, Edwin, *Death and the College Student* (A collection of brief essays on death and suicide), (New York: Behavioral Publications, 1972).

*Smith, Doris Buchanan, *A Taste of Blackberries* (New York: Thomas Y. Crowell Company, 1973).

"Thanatology 1: College Courses," *Time* (January 8, 1973), 101:36.

Ulanov, Barry, *Death: A Book of Preparation and Consolation* (New York: Sheed and Ward, 1959).

Vernon, Glenn M., *Sociology of Death: An Analysis of Death-Related Behavior* (New York: Ronald Press, 1970).

Weisman, Avery D., *On Dying and Denying: A Psychiatric Study of Terminality* (New York: Behavioral Publications, 1972).

Zim, Herbert S., and Sonia Bleeker, *Life and Death* (New York: William Morrow and Co., 1970).

4. THE FATHER'S ADJUSTMENT TO LIFE
AS A SINGLE PARENT

Biller, Henry B., *Father, Child and Sex Role* (Lexington, Mass.: D. C. Heath and Co., 1971).

Biller, Henry B., and Dennis Meredith, *Fathers and Children* (New York: McKay, 1975).

Bryan, James H., "Why Children Help: A Review," *Journal of Social Issues* (1972), 28:87–103.

Burchinal, L. G., "Characteristics of Adolescents from Unbroken, Broken, and Reconstituted Families," *Journal of Marriage and the Family* (1964), 26:44–50.

Burgess, Jane K., "The Single-Parent Family: A Social and Sociological Problem," *The Family Coordinator* (1970), 19:137–144.

Duberman, L., "Step-kin Relationships," *Journal of Marriage and the Family* (1973), 35:283–292.

Emmerich, Walter, "The Parental Role: A Functional-Cognitive Approach," *Monographs of the Society for Research in Child Development* (1969), 34:8.

Farrell, Warren, *The Liberated Man* (New York: Random House, 1975).

Fein, Robert A., "Men and Young Children," in *Men and Masculinity,* Joseph H. Pleck and Jack Sawyer, eds. (Englewood Cliffs, N.J.: Prentice-Hall/Spectrum Books, 1974), p. 54.

Gasser, Rita D., and Claribel M. Taylor, "Role Adjustment of Single Parent Fathers with Dependent Children," *The Family Coordinator* (1976), 25:397–401.

Hetherington, E. Mavis, "Effects of Father Absence on Personality Development in Adolescent Daughters," *Developmental Psychology* (1972), 7:313–326.

Jourard, Sidney M., "Some Lethal Aspects of the Male Role," in *Men and Masculinity,* Joseph H. Pleck and Jack Sawyer, eds. (Englewood Cliffs, N.J.: Prentice-Hall/Spectrum Books, 1974), p. 21.

Mendes, Helen A., "Single Fathers," *The Family Coordinator,* (1976), 25:434–444.

Orthner, Dennis K., and Terry Brown, "Single-Parent Fatherhood: An Emerging Family Life Style," *The Family Coordinator* (1976), 25:429–437.

Rosenberg, Benjamin G., and Brian Sutton-Smith, "Family Interaction Effects on Masculinity-femininity," *Journal of Personality and Social Psychology* (1968), 8:117–120.

Schlesinger, B., "The One-Parent Family: An Overview," *The Family Coordinator* (1966), 15:133–138.

Staub, Ervin A., "A Child in Distress: The Influence of Age and Number of Witnesses on Children's Attempts to Help," *Journal of Personality and Social Psychology* (1970), 14:130–140.

Stolz, Lois M., *Influences on Parent Behavior* (Stanford, Calif.: Stanford University Press, 1967).

Torrie, M., *Begin Again* (London: J. M. Dent, 1970).

Troll, Lillian E., "The Family of Later Life: A Decade Review," *Journal of Marriage and the Family* (1971), 33:263–290.

Walters, James, and Nick Stinnett, "Parent-child Relationships: A Decade Review of Research," *Journal of Marriage and the Family* (1971), 33:70–111.

Weiss, Robert S., "The Contributions of an Organization of Single Parents to the Well Being of Its Members," *The Family Coordinator* (1973), 22:321–326.

White, Burton L., and Jean C. Watts, *Experience and Environment: Major Influences on the Development of the Young Child* (Englewood Cliffs, N.J.: Prentice-Hall, 1973).

Whiting, Beatrice B., "Folk Wisdom and Child Rearing," *Merrill-Palmer Quarterly* (1974), 20:9–19.

5. THE WIDOWER'S REENTRANCE
INTO PAIRED SOCIETY

Berardo, Felix, "Survivorship and Social Isolation: The Case of the Aged Widower," *Family Coordinator* (1970), 19:11–25.

Bock, E. Wilbur, "Aging and Suicide: The Significance of Marital, Kinship, and Alternative Relations," *Family Coordinator* (1972), 21:71–79.

Bohannon, Paul, *Divorce and After* (Garden City, N.Y.: Doubleday, 1970).

Burgess, Jane K., "The Single-Parent Family: A Social and Sociological Problem," *Family Coordinator* (1970), 19:136–144.

Dullea, Georgia, "U.S. Statistics Show Single-Parent Families Growing 7 Times as Fast as 2-Parent Ones," *Toronto Globe and Mail* (December 4, 1974).

Goode, William, *Women in Divorce* (New York: Free Press, 1956).

Harvey, Carol D., and Howard Bahr, "Widowhood, Morale, and Affiliation," *Journal of Marriage and the Family* (1974), 36:97–106.

LeShan, Eda, *What Makes Me Feel This Way?* (New York: Macmillan, 1972).

Lopata, Helena Z., *Widowhood in an American City* (Cambridge, Mass.: Schenkman, 1973).

Mann, Peggy, *My Dad Lives in a Downtown Hotel* (New York: Doubleday, 1973).

Parkes, C. Murray, *Bereavement: Studies of Grief in Adult Life* (New York: International Universities, 1972).

Schlesinger, Ben, "The One-Parent Family in Canada: Some Recent Findings and Recommendations," *Family Coordinator* (1973) 22:305–309.

Silverman, Phyllis, "Widowhood and Preventive Intervention," *Family Coordinator* (1972), 21:95–102.

Sudia, Cecelia E., "An Updating and Comment on the United States Scene," *Family Coordinator* (1973), 22:309–311.

6. THE WIDOWER'S RETURN TO LIFE—
TO LOVE, ROMANCE AND SEX

Gallup, G., "Attitudes of Americans on Sex Seen Undergoing a Profound Change," Press release, August 1973, *Family Planning Digest* (1974), 3:1–3.

Hunt, Morton, *The World of the Formerly Married* (New York: McGraw-Hill, 1966).

Kogan, Benjamin, *Human Sexual Expression* (New York: Harcourt, Brace Jovanovich, 1973).

Komarovsky, Mirra, "Cultural Contradictions and Sex Roles: The Masculine Case," *American Journal of Sociology* (1973), 78: 111–122.

Masters, William, and Virginia Johnson, *Human Sexual Inadequacy* (Boston: Little, Brown and Co., 1970).

Masters, William, and Virginia Johnson *Human Sexual Response* (Boston: Little, Brown and Co., 1966).

McCary, James L., *Human Sexuality* (New York: D. Van Nostrand Co., 1973).

Reiss, Ira *The Social Context of Premarital Sexual Permissiveness* (New York: Holt, Rinehart & Winston, 1967).

Safilios-Rothschild, Constantina, *Love, Sex, and Sex Roles* (Englewood Cliffs, N.J.: Prentice-Hall, Inc., 1977).

7. THE CHOICE TO REMARRY OR REMAIN SINGLE

Bowlby, John, *Attachment and Loss: Vol. I, Attachment* (London: Hogarth, 1969).

Byrne, Donn, and William Griffitt, "Interpersonal Attraction," *Annual Review of Psychology* (1973), 24:317–336.

Fromm, Erich, *The Art of Loving* (New York: Harper & Row Pub. Inc., 1956).

Rogers, Carl R., *Becoming Partners: Marriage and Its Alternatives* (New York: Delacorte, 1972).

Stein, Peter J., *Single* (Englewood Cliffs, N.J.: Prentice-Hall, Inc., 1976).

8. REMARRIAGE—ITS PROBLEMS, ITS POSSIBILITIES

Ard, Ben N., Jr., "Communication in Marriage," *Rational Living* (1971), 5:220–22.

Atchley, Robert C., *The Social Forces in Later Life* (Belmont, Calif.: Wadsworth Publishing Co., Inc., 1972), p. 171.

Back, Kurt W., and Carleton S. Guptill, "Retirement and Self Ratings," in *Social Aspects of Aging,* Ida H. Simpson and John C. McKinney eds. (Durham, N.C.: Duke University Press, 1966), p. 129.

Bernard, Jessie, *Remarriage: A Study of Marriage* (New York: Dryden, 1956).

Blood, Robert O., and Donald Wolfe, *Husbands and Wives* (New York: Free Press, 1960).

Bowerman, C., and D. Irish, "Some Relationships of Stepchildren to Their Parents," *Marriage and Family Living* (1962), 24: 113–21.

Brownfield, E. Dorothy, "Communication: Key to Family Interaction," *Marriage and Family Living* (1953), 15:316–319.

Burchinal, L. D., "Characteristics of Adolescents from Unbroken, Broken, and Reconstituted Families," *Journal of Marriage and the Family* (1964), 26:44–50.

Burgess-Kohn, Jane, "A Note in Role Changes That Prepare Men for the Aging Process," in *The Wisconsin Sociologist,* vol. 13 (Spring-Summer 1976).

Burr, Wesley R., "Satisfaction with Various Aspects of Marriage over the Life Cycle: A Random Middle-Class Sample," *Journal of Marriage and the Family* (1970), 32:29–37.

Busse, Edward W., and Carl Eisdorfer, "Two Thousand Years of Married Life," in *Normal Aging,* Erdman Palmore, ed. (Durham, N.C.: Duke University Press, 1970).

Duberman, L., "Step-kin Relationships," *Journal of Marriage and the Family* (1973), 35:283–292.

165   Selected Bibliography

De Rosis, Helen, *Parent Power; Child Power* (New York: McGraw-Hill Book Co., 1974).

Duvall, Evelyn, *In-laws, Pro and Con* (New York: Association Press, 1954).

Erikson, Erik H., *Identity, Youth and Crisis* (New York: W. W. Norton and Co., Inc., 1968).

Farber, Bernard, "Family Organization and Crisis: Maintenance of Integration in Families," *Monographs of the Society for Research in Child Development* (1960), no. 25.

Figley, Charles, "Child Density and the Marital Relationship," *Journal of Marriage and the Family* (1973), 35:272–282.

Gillespie, Dair, "Who Has the Power? The Marital Struggle," *Journal of Marriage and the Family* (1971), 33:445–458.

Glenn, Norval A., "Psychological Well-being in the Postparental Stage; Some Evidence from National Surveys," *Journal of Marriage and the Family* (1975), 37:105–110.

Heath, Linda L., Brent S. Roper, and Charles D. King, "A Research Note on Children Viewed as Contributors to Marital Stability: The Relationship to Birth Control Use, Ideal, and Expected Family Size," *Journal of Marriage and the Family* (1974), 36:304–320.

Hill, Reuben, *Family Development in Three Generations* (Cambridge, Mass.: Schenkman, 1970).

Lipman, A., "Role Conceptions and Morale of Couples in Retirement," *Journal of Gerontology* (1961), 16:267–271.

Lobsenz, Norman, "Sex and the Senior Citizen," *New York Times Magazine* (January 1974), 8–9.

Luckey, Eleanor B., and Joyce K. Bain, "Children: A Factor in Marital Satisfaction," *Journal of Marriage and the Family* (1974), 32:43–44.

Maddox, B., *The Half-Parent* (New York: M. Evans, 1975).

Madsen, C., cited in David Knox, *Marriage Happiness: A Behavioral Approach to Counseling* (Champaign, Ill.: Research Press, 1972).

Masters, William H., and Virginia E. Johnson, *Human Sexual Response* (Boston: Little, Brown and Co., 1966), p. 269.

McCormick, M., *Stepfathers: What the Literature Reveals* (La Jolla, Calif.: Western Behavioral Sciences Institute, 1974).

Meriam, A. S., *The Stepfather in the Family* (Chicago: University of Chicago Press, 1940).

Miller, Sherod, Elam Nunnally, and Daniel B. Wackman, *Alive and Aware* (Minneapolis, Minn.: Interpersonal Communications Programs, Inc., 1975).

Rollings, E. M., "The Special Role of Stepfathers," *The Family Coordinator* (1976), 25:445–449.

Sawyer, Jack, "On Male Liberation," *Men and Masculinity* (Englewood Cliffs, N.J.: Prentice-Hall, Inc., 1974).

Safilios-Rothschild, Constantina, "The Dimensions of Power Distribution in the Family," in *Marriage Problems and Their Treatment*, Jacob Christ and Henry Grunebaum, eds. (Boston: Little, Brown and Co., 1972).

Schachter, Stanley, *The Psychology of Affiliation* (Stanford, Calif.: Stanford University Press, 1959).

Stinnett, Nick, Linda Mittelstet Carter, and James Montgomery, "Older Persons' Perceptions of Their Marriages," *Journal of Marriage and the Family* (1972), 34:665–680.

Sutton-Smith, Brian, and Benjamin G. Rosenberg, *The Sibling* (New York: Holt, Rinehart & Winston, 1970).

Terman, Lewis M., *Psychological Factors in Marital Happiness* (New York: McGraw-Hill, 1938).

Whiting, Beatrice B., "Folk Wisdom and Child Rearing," *Merrill-Palmer Quarterly* (1974), 20:9–19.

Wilson, K., L. A. Zurcher, D. C. McAdams, and R. L. Curtis, "Stepfathers and Stepchildren: An Exploratory Analysis from Two National Surveys," *Journal of Marriage and the Family* (1975), 37:526–536.

Wohlford, Paul, John W. Santrock, Stephen Berger, and David Liberman, "Older Brothers' Influence on Sex-Typed, Aggressive, and Dependent Behavior in Father-Absent Children," *Developmental Psychology* (1971), 4:124–134.

INDEX

Abandonment, child's feeling of: 62
Abstinence: 103
Acceptance of reality: 37
Adjusting: to loss, 38; to remarriage, 138–139
Advice: from widowers, 95, 115–116; helpful, 37
Alcohol and sex: 109
Alone: in decision, 19, 24; in grief, 26, 27
American Association of Sex Educators and Counselors: 104
Anger: reaction to death, 24; slowing recovery of bereaved, 35; at sudden death, 36; reaction of children, 54
Antidepressant drugs: 39
Authority, parental: 139
Avoidance by friends: 85
Avoidance of topic of death: 64

Bereavement: 27–28

Change: necessity for in remarriage, 142; resisting, 83, 112
Cheating, feeling of: 100
Child care, sources of: 78
Child and family centers: 78
Children and remarriage, 79–80; denial in grieving, 53; discussing death with, 63; hardship of watching death process, 21; learning of death, 45, 47, 49, 50; learning of incurability, 7, 9; with new mother, 121–122
Comfort for bereaved teenager: 56, 64–65
Comfort of loving friends: 24
Communication in family: 65, 75, 151
Companionship, need for: 84, 89, 95
Conversation, adult: 90
Coping with death, one child's way: 64–65

Counseling: 38; for family, 134; how to find, 41; sexual, 103, 110. *See also* Organizations for widowed.
Crying: children's reaction to parental, 46; deciding on treatment, 19; encouraging for boys, 59–60; gratitude and sorrow, 18; learning of death, 24; with children, 42, 66

Dating: 83–84; advice from widowers, 95; and guilt, 73, 100–101; good taste in beginning, 96; problems with young children, 96; problems with grownup children, 98
Daughters, dealing with: 75
Death education: 86
Denial of grief: 29, 35; in children, 53
Depression: and impotency, 103; indications of, 38
Despair: at grave, 26; of loneliness, 35
Disbelief: reaction to death, 24; sense of, 36
Discussing death with children: 63
Doubt. *See* Self-doubt
Drinking, potential problem: 98, 130, 150
Dying, patient responses to: 16

Elderly widower, special problems of: 116, 148
Emotional reactions of bereavement: 52
Emotional stress: 37
Emotions: pent-up, 29; venting, 9, 37
Empathy needed: in grieving, 28; from psychiatrist, 39; for stepmother, 128
Emptiness, feeling of: 12, 15
Experience, asset in remarriage: 148